MarketSim

Student Manual

Prepared by

Rochelle L. Ruffer
Youngstown State University

and

Ebenge Usip
Youngstown State University

THOMSON

SOUTH-WESTERN

Australia · Canada · Mexico · Singapore · Spain · United Kingdom · United States

THOMSON

SOUTH-WESTERN

Student Manual to accompany MarketSim

Prepared by
Rochelle L. Ruffer and Ebenge Usip

Vice President / Editorial Director:
Jack W. Calhoun

Vice President / Editor-in-Chief:
Dave Shaut

Publisher of Economics:
Michael B. Mercier

Sr. Acquisitions Editor - Economics:
Peter Adams

Developmental Editor:
Jennifer E. Baker

Sr. Marketing Manager:
John Carey

Sr. Marketing Coordinator:
Jenny Garamy

Production Editor:
Daniel C. Plofchan

Sr. Manufacturing Coordinator:
Sandee Milewski

Manager of Technology, Editorial:
Vicky True

Technology Project Manager:
John Barans

Compositor:
OffCenter Concept House
Soldotna, AK

Cover Designer:
Bethany Casey

Cover Photographer/Illustrator:
© PhotoDisc,Inc

Printer:
Westgroup
Eagan, MN

Package ISBN:
0-324-22205-X

Book ISBN:
0-324-22207-6

Access Card ISBN:
0-324-31977-0

Questionnaire ISBN:
0-324-32017-5

For permission to use
material from this text or
product, submit a request
online at
http://www.thomsonrights.com.

Any additional questions
about permissions can be
submitted by email to
thomsonrights@thomson.com.

TABLE OF CONTENTS

Introduction to MarketSim

Welcome to MarketSim! The goal of this program is to let you participate in a simulated economy to help you better understand how economic systems work. MarketSim is accessed via the Internet, so you can participate in the simulation from anywhere you have Internet access.

MarketSim consists of two parts: Jeremy's Market and Adam's Market. In Jeremy's Market each student is responsible for a household that consumes and produces goods. You also will be able to trade with the households run by your classmates. Your goal is to try to pick a production and trading strategy that gives your household the highest possible level of happiness.

In Adam's Market you will be responsible for both a household and a firm, and money is used to make transactions between firms and households. As a household, you need to decide how many hours you are going to work and what goods you will buy. As a firm, you need to decide how much labor time to hire and how much output to produce. In more complex versions of the simulation, you will also need to decide whether to make additional investments in your firm's capital and whether to switch industries. Your goals are to try to maximize your household's happiness and the value of your firm.

Our hope is that participating in MarketSim will challenge you to try to apply the concepts you are learning in class and make Economics come alive for you. Let the trading begin!

Minimum System Requirements & Site Access

MINIMUM SYSTEM REQUIREMENTS

To participate in MarketSim your computer must be running one of the following Microsoft Windows operating systems: Windows 98, Me, 2000, XP Home, or XP Pro. In addition, it must meet the following minimum system requirements:

- Pentium Processor with 200 MHz clock speed. (Recommended: At least a Pentium II Processor with 266 MHz clock speed, or similar processor standard such as Cyrix 333.)
- Internet Explorer 5.x
- Flash Player 5.0 plug-in (to view the Getting Started tutorial)
- 32 MB RAM (Recommended: At least 64 MB)
- Mouse
- Video display capable of 256 colors (16-bit color recommended) and 800 x 600 resolution
- Sound card with 8-bit audio capabilities (to hear the Getting Started tutorial).
- Internet connection with a speed of 56K or higher.

Information about Netscape

The 7.x and higher versions of Netscape will likely work well for using this site, with the exception of probable sub-par performance in displaying the graphs on the Consumer / Graphs page, the Firm / Graphs page, the Consumer Worksheet graphs, and the Firm Labor Worksheet graphs (all of which are Java applets). However, Netscape is not advertised here as a supported browser.

Information about the Macintosh Platform

Using Netscape 7.x and higher, the Macintosh platform (OS 9.1 and higher) will likely work well for using this site, with the exception of possible problems in displaying graphs. However, the Macintosh platform is not advertised here as a supported browser.

Student access to the MarketSim web site is granted in two steps.

1. In your Student Manual there will be a Student Access Code. Go to the http://marketsim.swlearning.com web site, click on the <Register an Access Code> link, and use your access code to create a User Name and Password combination. You will then be redirected to the MarketSim Student Log In page.
2. On the Student Log In page, you will submit your User Name / Password combination, and will then land on your "Account" page.

SITE ACCESS

The Front Door

The web address http://marketsim.swlearning.com will display the MarketSim "front door." The major front door options are shown in Figure 1.

Figure 1: A Partial View the MarketSim "Front Door"

What is MarketSim?

Curious?
<u><Find Out></u>

Try a demonstration version of
MarketSim.
<u><Go></u>

Instructors

Already registered?
<u><Log In></u>

Not registered?
<u><Register></u>

Students

Already registered?
<u><Log In></u>

Not registered but have an
access code?
<u><Register an Access Code></u>

Purchase Student Manual and
access to MarketSim.
<u><Purchase></u>

WHAT IS MARKETSIM?

What is MarketSim?

The <Find Out> link opens a page with a description of the program and the advantages of using it. The <Go> link leads to a Flash demo that gives an overview of MarketSim and links to demos showing how the program works.If you have problems loading this Flash demo you should update the Flash Player (for free) at:
<u>http://www.macromedia.com/shockwave/download/download.cgi?P1_Prod_Version=ShockwaveFlash</u>.

INSTRUCTORS

Instructors

These options will be of no interest to you, since you will not be able to register as an instructor.

STUDENTS

Students

Let's start from the bottom of these options and work higher.

- *<Purchase>*. Because you are reading this Student Manual, we will assume that you don't need to know how to go through the <Purchase> system to purchase the Student Manual and its student access code for accessing the MarketSim web site. Just understand that should you want to buy another Student Manual, this <Purchase> avenue is a convenient way to do so.

- *<Register an Access Code>* If you have an access code that you have not registered, click here to do so. Details on this registration process are provided later in this document. Note that you should be careful with this access code. It can only be used one time. If someone else obtains your access code and uses it, then you will not be able to use it. Also note that if you have a used Student Manual, the access code might be invalid. The access code to access MarketSim online is only available with the purchase of a new Student Manual.

- *<Log In>* If you have previously turned an access code into a User Name and Password combination, click <Log In> to submit that combination for access to your "Account" page and the MarketSim games available to you on that page. Details on this log in process are provided later in this document.

Registering an Access Code

THE FIRST SCREEN

After you click on the <Register an Access Code> link the content shown in Figure 2 will appear.

Figure 2: A Partial View of the First Screen for Registering an Access Code

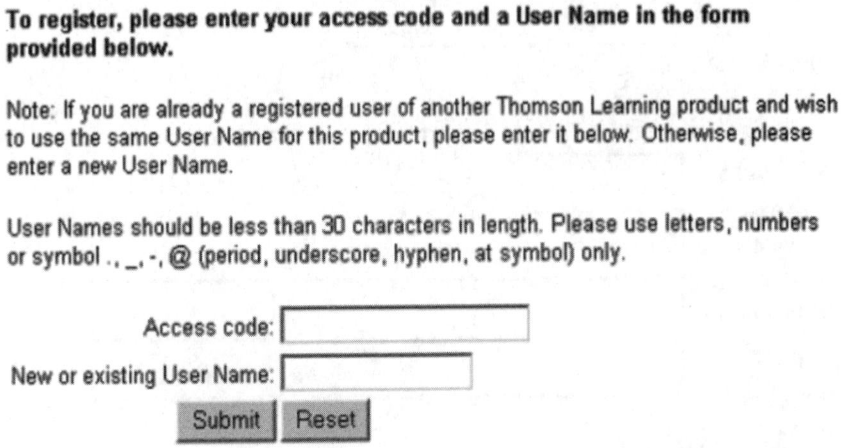

To register, please enter your access code and a User Name in the form provided below.

Note: If you are already a registered user of another Thomson Learning product and wish to use the same User Name for this product, please enter it below. Otherwise, please enter a new User Name.

User Names should be less than 30 characters in length. Please use letters, numbers or symbol ., _, -, @ (period, underscore, hyphen, at symbol) only.

Access code: [   ]

New or existing User Name: [   ]

Submit   Reset

1. In the "Access code:" field, enter the access code you received with your Student Manual.
2. In the "New or existing User Name:" field, enter your desired user name, taking into account the user name rules that are shown above the two data entry fields in Figure 2. Why does the label mention the possibility of an "existing" User Name? If you have a User Name that you use for other Thomson Learning products, such as Personal Trainer, Interactive Text, MBA Primer, Certification Preparation or Review, etc., for simplicity, you can use the same User Name. Otherwise, submit a new User Name.
3. Submit this information.

THE SECOND SCREEN

After you successfully submit your access code and User Name, the content shown in Figure 3 will appear.

Figure 3: A Partial View of the Second Screen for Registering an Access Code

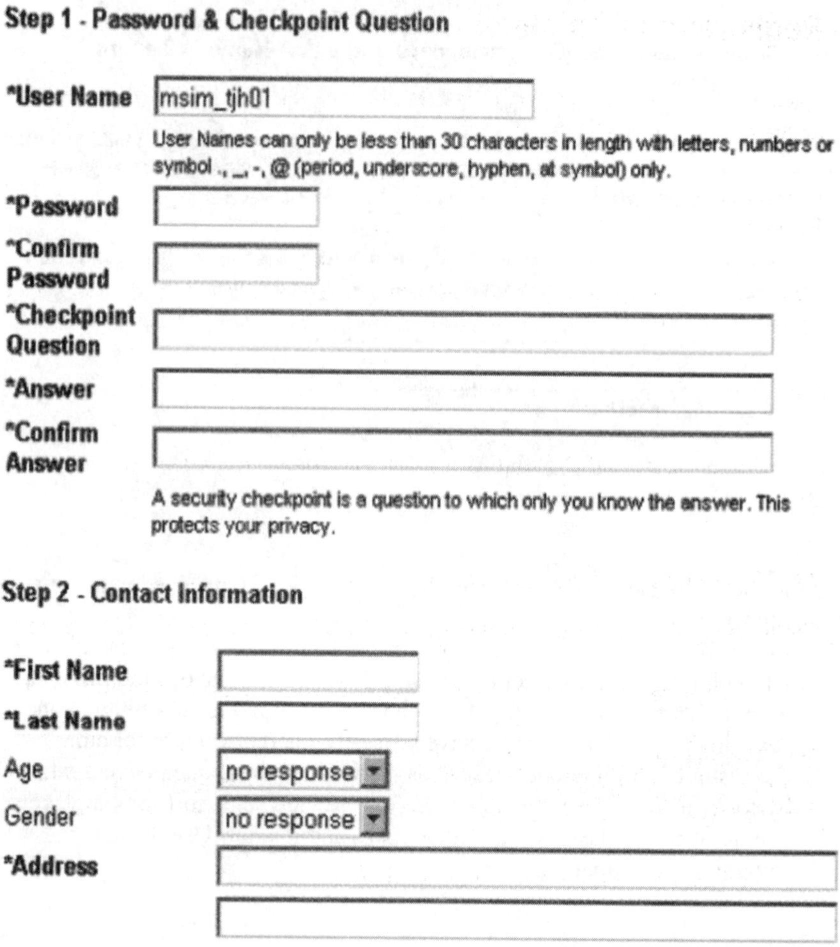

Step 1 - Password & Checkpoint Question

*User Name `msim_tjh01`

User Names can only be less than 30 characters in length with letters, numbers or symbol ., _, -, @ (period, underscore, hyphen, at symbol) only.

*Password

*Confirm Password

*Checkpoint Question

*Answer

*Confirm Answer

A security checkpoint is a question to which only you know the answer. This protects your privacy.

Step 2 - Contact Information

*First Name

*Last Name

Age   no response ▼

Gender   no response ▼

*Address

1. Enter all required information.
2. At the bottom of this (long) form, click the Submit button to submit this information.

THE THIRD SCREEN

After you successfully submit the information on the second screen, the content shown in Figure 4 will appear.

Figure 4: A Partial View of the Third Screen for Registering an Access Code

Registration Complete!

Thank you for registering for South-Western's MarketSim. Your registration will be valid for the next 365 days.

User Name: msim_tjh01
Password: msim_tjh01

Please record this information for future reference. Your registration information will also be sent in an email message to the email address you provided: hilts@rapidnet.com.

Click Here to access your registered product.

If you are not automatically redirected to the MarketSim Student Log In screen, click the Here link to travel there.

The Student Log In Process

The most significant portion of the Student Log In screen is shown in Figure 5.

Figure 5: A Partial View of the Student Log In Screen

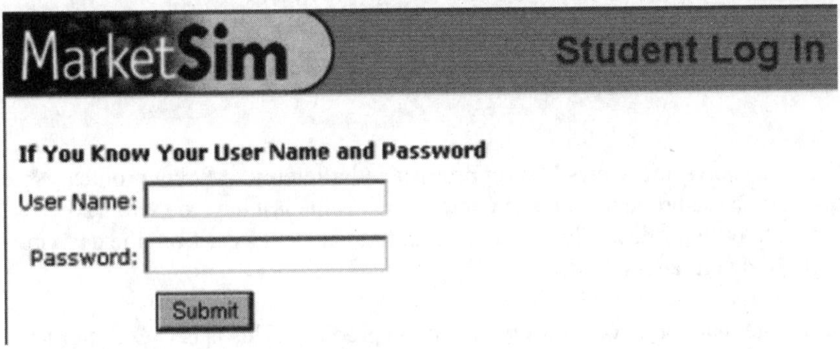

Enter your User Name and Password, and click the Submit button. One of two things will happen.

- If your User Name and Password combination is not recognized by MarketSim, the following error text will appear on the screen.

  The User Name/Password combination you provided does not correspond with any non-expired MarketSim products. Please check it and try again (making sure that you use capital and lowercase letters as you did when you originally created your Password). If you have forgotten your User Name and/or Password, click here for a reminder.

If this happens, use the click here for a reminder link. If problems persist, contact Thomson Learning Technical Support at 800-423-0563.

- Or, if your User Name and Password combination is recognized, you will be taken to your student Account page.

The Student Account Page

The most significant portion of the Student Log In screen is shown in Figure 6.

Figure 6: Partial View of the Student Account Page the First Time a Student Sees It

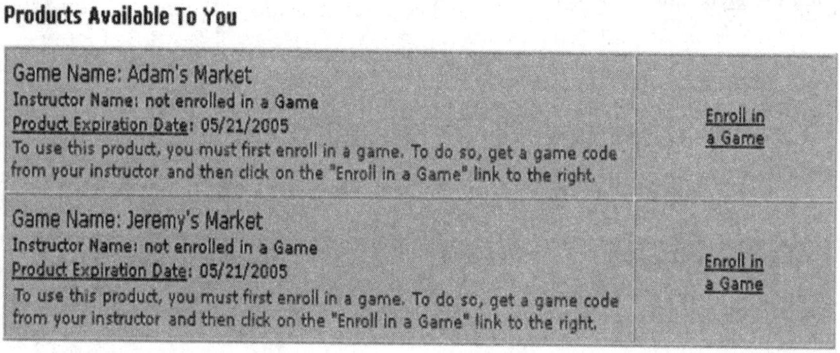

Products Available To You

Game Name: Adam's Market Instructor Name: not enrolled in a Game Product Expiration Date: 05/21/2005 To use this product, you must first enroll in a game. To do so, get a game code from your instructor and then click on the "Enroll in a Game" link to the right.	Enroll in a Game
Game Name: Jeremy's Market Instructor Name: not enrolled in a Game Product Expiration Date: 05/21/2005 To use this product, you must first enroll in a game. To do so, get a game code from your instructor and then click on the "Enroll in a Game" link to the right.	Enroll in a Game

Figure 6 shows an Adam's Market product and a Jeremy's Market product. Note that each has a product expiration date, which is the last day you will have access to each product. The product expiration date is 1 year from the day you registered your access code.

Also note that you have no way to open the products. This is because in order to use a product you must first turn it into a "game" by enrolling it in a game. Details on game enrollment are provided in the next section.

ENROLL IN A GAME

When you click on the Enroll in a Game link, a window will open with the content shown in Figure 7.

Figure 7: Partial View of the Enroll in a Game Window for Jeremy's Market

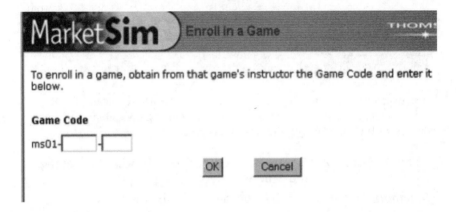

Note the required "Game Code." This is something that your instructor will provide to you, and submitting it will link you into the game the instructor has set up for your class. A successful game code submission will close the "Enroll in a Game" window and will update your Account page as is shown in Figure 8.

Figure 8: Partial View of the Student Account Page, after Enrolling the Jeremy's Market Game, but Not Yet Enrolled in the Adam's Market Game

Products Available To You

Game Name: Adam's Market		
Instructor Name: not enrolled in a Game Product Expiration Date: 05/21/2005 To use this product, you must first enroll in a game. To do so, get a game code from your instructor and then click on the "Enroll in a Game" link to the right.	Enroll in a Game	
Game Name: Jeremy's Market		
Instructor Name: Tom Hilt Product Expiration Date: 05/21/2005 This game will not begin until 6/24/04 at 11:00 A.M. Eastern. Until then, you cannot enter the game.	Change Game	Drop Game

OK, so now you've enrolled in a game. Why don't you yet have a way to open the game? Well, your instructor determines the date and time at which the game will begin, and you may not enter that game until it has started. Figure 8 assumes that you enrolled in a game that has not yet started. What would you see if the game had started? When you return to the Student Account page after the game has started, you will see what is shown in Figure 9.

Figure 9: A Jeremy's Market Row on the Student Account Page, for a Jeremy's Market Game That Has Begun

Game Name: Jeremy's Market Open It Edit Name
Instructor Name: Tom Hilt   Change   Drop
Product Expiration Date: 05/21/2005   Game   Game
This game is currently in Period 1 of 6. Period 3 will end 6/30/04 at 11:00 A.M. Eastern.

So, between Figures 8 and 9 you can see three of the different states for games on the student Account page. Table 1 shows the other six possible game states. For all six states, the Open It link will not be visible.

Table 1: Additional Status Possibilities for a Product or Game on the Student Account Page

Situation: The game is active, but the instructor has paused it.
Status Message: Your instructor has paused this game, and you will not be able to enter it again until the instructor resumes it.
Situation: The game is active, but the instructor has blocked you for some reason.
Status Message: The instructor of {Game Name} has blocked you from the game, making you ineligible from joining that game. Contact your instructor if you believe that you have been blocked in error. You may also enroll in a different game, if you have a Game Code from an instructor.
Situation: The Game Is Active, but You Tried to Enroll after It Began (a "Late Enrollment")
Status Message: The instructor of {Game Name} has not yet responded to your enrollment application, and you will not be granted entrance to that game until the instructor approves your application.
Additional Information: If you try to enroll before a game begins, you receive automatic enrollment. If you try to enroll after a game begins, the instructor receives your application and must admit you or deny you manually.
Situation: Instructor Approves "Late Enrollment"
Status Message: The instructor of {Game Name} has approved your enrollment application! Click on the "Open It" link to enter the game.
Situation: Instructor Denies "Late Enrollment"
Status Message: The instructor of {Game Name} has denied your enrollment application. You may, though enroll in a different game, if you have a Game Code from an instructor. OK

> **Situation:** The Game Has Concluded
> **Status Message:** This game has ended. You can open the simulation to review your experience,
> but you will not be able to perform any actions. OK

CHANGE GAME AND DROP GAME

You can drop a game at any time. This will return you to the state shown for the Adam's Market product in Figure 8. You can also change game at any time. This requires that you have a game code for a different game. Be sure to note the game code for the game you are leaving, in the event that you want to return to it later. Note, though, that if you try to return to a game that you have left, this will be considered a late enrollment, and the instructor who manages the game you are trying to revisit will need to manually accept or deny your enrollment application.

OPEN IT

A Jeremy's Market "Open It" link will open the Jeremy's Market game in a new window. An Adam's Market "Open It" link will open the Adam's Market game in a new window. Details on both of these types of games are discussed later in this Manual.

LOGOUT, TIMEOUT, PERIOD CHANGE, AND PAUSE GAME

Imagine that you are in either an Adam's Market game or a Jeremy's Market game and you leave the game open while you enjoy a 30-minute lunch break. Because MarketSim "times out" after 20 minutes of inactivity, when you return to the game and click on some link or button, MarketSim will throw an alert at you, cancel your session, and close the game and all windows opened from the game. This will mean that the only MarketSim window you will see open will be your Account Page. After this has happened, any link you click on the Account page will take you to the screen shown in Figure 10.

Figure 10: A Partial View of the Redirect Screen after Loss of Session

Your current session in MarketSim has expired and you will need to log in to your account once more. To do so, click here.

This unusual response for a click on one of the Account page links will occur whenever a session has been lost. Sessions are lost due to logout (which is your request to end your session), timeout, period change, and pause game. These situations are described in more detail later in this document.

Jeremy's Market: A Barter Economy

INTRODUCTION

The Jeremy's Market section of the manual is divided into three parts.

I.   The first part is this brief Introduction.

II. The second part gives an overview of Jeremy's Market, offers some tips on strategy, and gives descriptions of each component of the program. Much of this information is also available through the simulation's Help system.

III. The third part of the Jeremy's Market coverage will present a number of activities and exercises that relate Jeremy's Market to the economic theory you are learning in class. The activities are designed to help you better understand the key concepts of scarcity, choice, and opportunity cost in relation to production, consumption, and trade.

OVERVIEW, STRATEGY TIPS, AND PROGRAM STRUCTURE

Overview

In Jeremy's Market you and each of the classmates in your game are responsible for a household, and your goal is to maximize your household's happiness. Each household consumes two goods. Your household's happiness, or utility in the jargon of economics, depends on your household's consumption of the two goods and leisure time.

The game is divided into periods. In each period of the game every household has use of 100 hours. During each period you can spend some of your time producing goods and retain some hours to enjoy as leisure time. You can also trade the goods you produce with other participants during the period.

At the end of the period the program will calculate your utility based on the goods you have in stock and the time that was retained for leisure. Your challenge is to try to use your time to maximize the amounts you consume and balance your consumption of the goods to make your household as happy as possible.

The following provides a quick summary of the rules of a Jeremy's Market game:

- Before actually starting Jeremy's Market, you will first land on Jeremy's Island where you have the task of maximizing utility without trade.
- Once you leave Jeremy's Island and start Jeremy's Market, the game will be divided into some number of periods set by your instructor.
- At the beginning of each period, the number of units consumed is set to zero and each household is given an allotment of time (usually 100 hours).
- You and your classmates will be divided into "attribute groups." All of the members of an attribute group have the same utility and production functions.
- When you produce units of a good or receive units of a good in trade, those units are added to your stock of that good. All the units in stock at the end of the period are consumed.
- Your utility is a function of the goods you consume and the amount of time you have retained for leisure.
- To trade goods, you can either accept an offer posted by another student or post your own offer and wait to see if another student accepts the offer.

- You can cancel an offer to trade if it has not yet been accepted by another student.
- Any offers that have not been accepted at the end of the period expire and are removed from the list of available offers.
- It is possible to trade time. If you receive time in a trade you are essentially hiring another student to work for you, and you must chose what would be produced with the time. You cannot consume another student's time as leisure time.
- You will be assigned points based on the number of periods you participate in and your total utility (the sum of your utility from all of the periods).

Strategy Tips

- On Jeremy's Island, try to produce and consume so that you are getting the same additional utility from the last hour spent on each good (the values for MUxMP should be equal, or MRS should equal the tradeoff in production, depending on the approach to consumer choice your instructor has chosen).
- Once you enter Jeremy's market, you have no idea what trades other participants are likely to accept. It is a good idea to initially produce relatively small amounts of both goods and offer to trade the good that are better at producing.
- When barter is possible, try to accumulate a bundle of goods so that you get the same additional utility from the last dollar spent on each good given the implicit prices of the goods (if your instructor is describing consumer choice in terms of marginal utility), or so that the tradeoff between goods is the same as the relative prices (if your instructor is describing consumer choice in terms of the MRS).

Program Structure

JEREMY'S ISLAND (A SELF-SUFFICIENT, OR ROBINSON CRUSOE ECONOMY)

When you first open a Jeremy's Market game, you will land on "Jeremy's Island" (see Figure 11). Consider yourself being briefly stranded on the island so you cannot trade with anyone—you can only consume the goods that you yourself produce. To get off the island, you must find the highest level of utility you can achieve when you cannot trade. Try using the two tables on the Jeremy's Island page to select the combination of leisure, bread, and wine that gives you the highest possible utility, and then press the button marked "Check

Answer." If you find the correct combination you will leave the island and join other participants in Jeremy's Market.

Figure 11: Jeremy's Island Screen

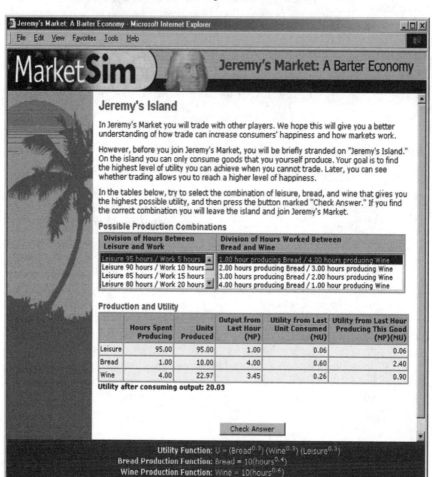

The individual tables on this page are described as follows.

Possible Production Combinations
The left-hand side of the table lists different possible divisions between the number of hours consumed as leisure time and the total number of hours spent producing the goods. (Note that in this Manual the two goods are referred to as bread and wine—the default names. Your instructor might choose different names for your game.) The right-hand side of the table lists the possible

combinations of time spent producing bread and the time spent producing wine given the total number of hours spent working.

Production and Utility

As you select different combinations, the program calculates the number of units of bread and wine that will be produced and displays the results in the Production and Utility table. The information you are given will depend on the utility-maximizing rule that you are using.

- **Production and Utility, MU** If you are discussing consumer choice in terms of marginal utility, the program will calculate marginal product, marginal utility, and the product of those two values. Marginal product times marginal utility (MPxMU) will tell you how much utility you will receive when you spend an additional hour producing a good and consuming the output.

- **Production and Utility, MRS** If you are discussing consumer choice in terms of the marginal rate of substitution, the program will calculate the MRS for each pair of goods. It will also calculate the tradeoff in production of each pair of goods—the amount of one good that would have to be given up to produce one more unit of another good. The tradeoff in production is equal to the slope of the production possibilities frontier. To maximize utility you want to have the tradeoff in production equal to the MRS for each pair of goods.

Try different combinations of work, leisure, bread, and wine to find the utility-maximizing mix. Then press the button labeled "Check Answer." After the program has confirmed that you have found the utility-maximizing combination, click on the "Set Sail" button to gain access to Jeremy's Market.

JEREMY'S MARKET: A BARTER ECONOMY

Page Design

All of the pages in Jeremy's Market have the same basic design (see Figure 12). The black bar across the top underneath the title is referred to as the **top navigation bar**. The links on it open separate windows for the **Worksheet** and **Help** pages, while the **Logout** link simply displays a message asking you to confirm that you really want to log out.

The **Worksheet** is used to plan your strategy as a consumer and is described in detail below. Clicking on **Help** will open a window that displays information about the page you are currently viewing and provides access to Help pages for other parts of the program.

The blue panel (note that all screens in this manual are printed in black and white; colors noted here are as they will appear on your computer screen in the simulation) on the left side of the screen is referred to as the **left navigation panel** with links to the **Actions**, **Functions**, **Graphs**, and **Record** pages. All of the pages are described in detail later in this Manual.

The dark blue bar across the bottom of the page is referred to as a **ticker panel**. The ticker panel includes the following information: your utility for the current period and your total utility from all periods, the number of hours you have spent producing goods and the time remaining that can be used for leisure, and your stocks of bread and wine. Your current utility is equal to what your utility would be if you consumed the goods you currently have in stock.

Figure 12: Jeremy's Market Screen

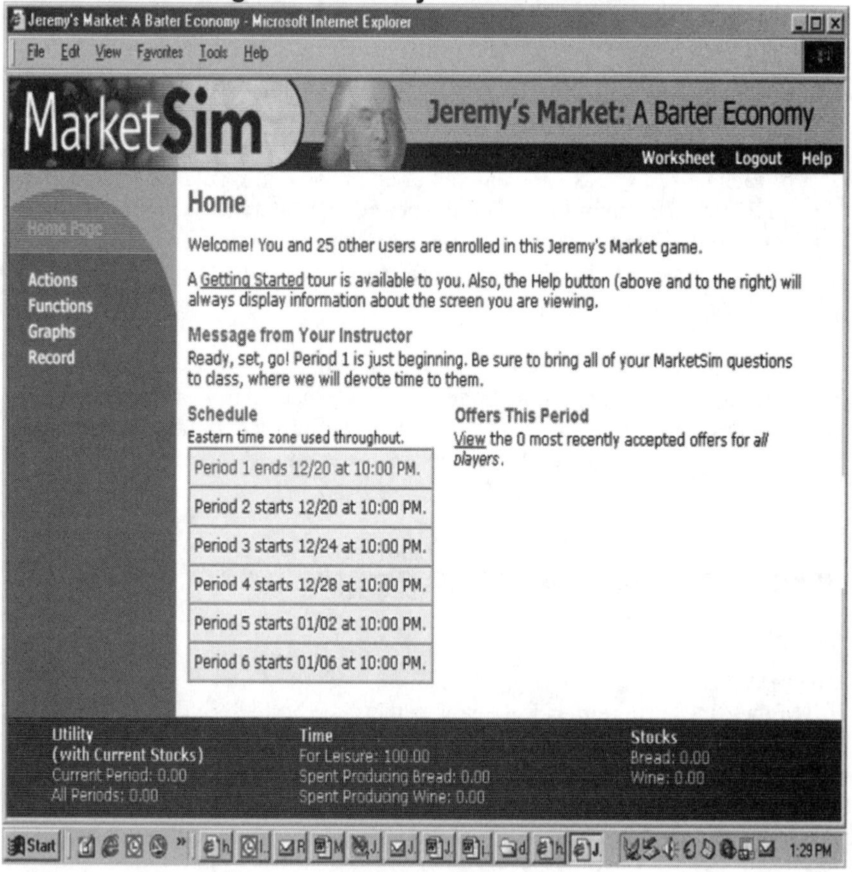

Home Page

Whenever you enter Jeremy's Market the first page that is displayed is the **Home Page**, which provides some general information about what has been going on in the game (see Figure 12). On the home page you can see how many players are registered to participate in your game, a message from your instructor, and the timeline for the periods in the game. You can also view a list of your offers that were accepted since you last logged into the game and a list of recently accepted offers by all students.

The page also contains a link titled "Getting Started." If you click on this link the program will display a description of the simulation and strategy tips. We strongly encourage you to click on the "Getting Started" link the first time you use Jeremy's Market.

Worksheet

Clicking on the Worksheet link on the top navigation bar opens a separate window for the Worksheet (see Figure 13). As noted earlier, the Worksheet is provided to help you plan your strategy. You will actually produce and trade goods using the other pages. The different parts of the Worksheet are described on the following pages.

Figure 13: Worksheet

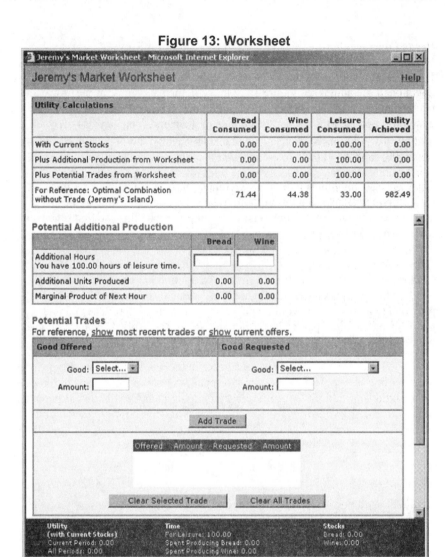

Utility Calculations

The Utility Calculations table allows you to see how your utility would change as you take different actions. The first row of the table shows what you currently have in stock and what your utility would be if you took no additional actions.

The second row reflects your input from the "Potential Additional Production Table." For example, assume you had 40 units of bread in stock, and you now indicate that you want to spend two more hours producing bread in the "Potential Additional Production Table." The additional bread that would be produced, let's say 20 loaves, would be added to your stock of bread, and your leisure time would be reduced by two hours. Your utility in the second row would be recalculated using the higher consumption of bread and the reduction in leisure. This allows you to determine whether you can increase your utility by producing more output.

The third row of the table reflects both your input from the "Potential Additional Production" table and the table labeled "Potential Trades." For example, suppose in the "Potential Trades" table you traded 10 units of bread for 10 units of wine. The values in the third row would reflect both the additional production and the proposed trade. This allows you to see whether a specific trade will cause your utility to rise.

The final row of the table shows the optimal combination from Jeremy's Island, the utility-maximizing combination when trade is not possible. Your utility with trade should never be less than your Jeremy's Island utility.

Potential Additional Production

This section allows you to experiment with how your utility will change if you spend additional hours producing one or more of the goods. The calculations take into account how much time you have already spent producing the goods and how much you have already consumed. In the text boxes you can type in the number of additional hours you want to spend producing a good and the amount that would be produced is then displayed below. The table will also display the additional output you would create if you spent another hour producing that good. As noted earlier, the effect of the additional output on your utility will be displayed in the second row of the Utility Calculations table.

Potential Trades

In this section you can see how making trades will effect your utility. Use the dropdown menus to indicate what you would like to trade away and what you would like to receive in trade. Fill in the amounts in the text boxes and click the button labeled "Add Trade." The effect of the trade will be added to the Utility Calculations table, and you can see how your utility would change with the trade. Clicking the "Clear Selected Trade" button removes the trades.

To view the most recent trades or current offers click on the links labeled **show**. Clicking the first **show** link allows you to see the exchange rates for the last five trades, while clicking on the second **show** link allows you to see all current offers. For example, if 15 units of wine were traded for 10 units of bread, then the exchange rate of wine for bread would be equal to 1.5 (on average, the trader gave up 1.5 units of wine for every unit of bread received). You will want to view these tables so you have some idea of the trades you will be able to make.

Utility Maximization

Scroll down the window to display the Utility Maximization table. This table will take one of two forms, depending on the rule for utility maximization your class is using. In both cases the table is used to help you decide whether you are consuming the best possible mix of goods.

- *Utility Maximization, MU per Dollar* Type in values for the exchange rates, and then press the button labeled "Calculate MU per Dollar." The program will calculate the implicit prices of the goods based on the exchange rates you specified. It will also calculate the marginal utility per last dollar spent (MU/P). To maximize utility, you should be receiving the same additional utility per dollar spent on each good.

- *Production and Utility, MRS* Type in values for the exchange rates and then press the button labeled "Calculate MRS." The program will calculate the MRS for all three possible pairs of the goods. You will want to compare the values of the marginal rates of substitution to the exchange rates for the different goods. At the utility-maximizing combination your MRS for each pair of goods should be close to the exchange rate for that pair.

Production Possibilities Frontiers/Indifference Curves

Clicking on the drop-down menu will display a list of the possible combinations of bread, wine and leisure. Select a combination to generate the graph along with the indifference curve passing through the combination that you have selected. It will also display a consumption opportunity curve, which shows the different consumption options available to you given any trades you have made. If you have not made any trades the consumption opportunity curve and the production possibilities curve will be the same.

Actions

Produce Goods

This section of the Actions page allows you to produce additional output. As shown in Figure 14 there are two text boxes where you can type in the additional amount of time you want to spend producing the two goods. Also displayed is the number of hours currently allocated to leisure, which is the maximum number of hours that could be used for production. Remember that you do not want to use all of your leisure time to produce goods because leisure also contributes to your happiness.

Figure 14: Actions / Produce Goods

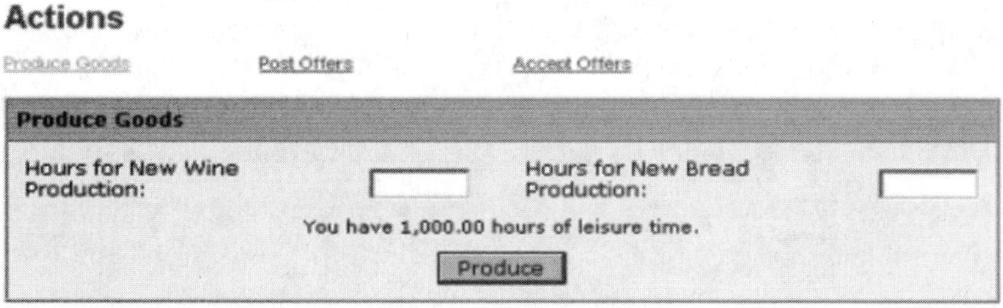

Actions

Produce Goods   Post Offers   Accept Offers

Produce Goods

| Hours for New Wine Production: | [   ] | Hours for New Bread Production: | [   ] |

You have 1,000.00 hours of leisure time.

[Produce]

To produce more of a good, type in the number of additional hours you want to spend producing the good in the text box and click on the button labeled "Produce."

Post Offers

In this section of the Actions page you can post offers to trade goods and time with other players in your game (see Figure 15). Select the good you are offering to trade from the drop-down menu. Type the number of units you want to trade away immediately below.

In the right-hand side of the box, select the good that you want to receive in trade, and type the number of units you are asking for in the text box. Note that if you receive time, you must indicate which good is to be produced with the time you receive. The amount of output produced will be determined by your production function and the amount of time you have already spent producing the good this period. When you are receiving time to trade you are in effect hiring another player to work for you to produce the output.

Figure 15: Actions / Post Offers

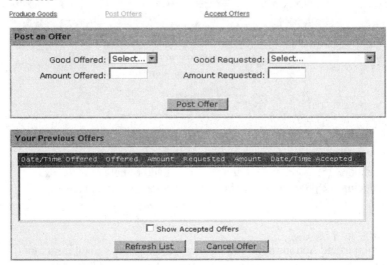

Press the button marked "Post Offer" button to add your offer to the list of available offers. You now need to wait and see if someone accepts your offer. At this point you may want to exit the game and check back a few hours later.

At the end of a period, all offers that were not accepted are canceled.

If you post an offer and no one accepts it after a reasonable amount of time, you might want to cancel the offer and post a new one. For example, suppose you offered to trade 10 units of bread for 20 units of wine. No one accepted your offer, and in the most recent trades one unit of bread was typically traded for one unit of wine. You might choose to cancel the offer, and then post a new offer to trade 10 units of bread for 10 units of wine.

The list box displays all of the offers you have posted which have not been accepted. To cancel an offer, simply select it from the list of the displayed trades and click on the "Cancel Offer" button. To cancel all trades in the list, select them and then click on "Clear All Trades".

Accept Offers
In this section of the Actions page you can accept offers to trade made by other players (see Figure 16). Click on the radio button of the item you want to receive in a trade, select an offer, and click on the button labeled "Accept Offer." Clicking on the button labeled "Refresh List" asks the program to check to see if any additional offers have been posted since you moved to the Accept Offers page.

Figure 16: Actions / Accept Offers

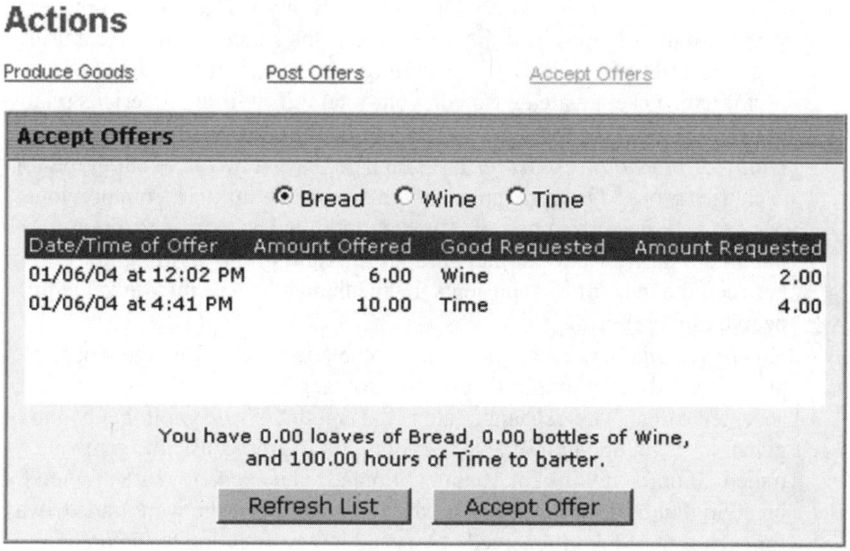

Actions

Produce Goods   Post Offers   Accept Offers

Accept Offers

⊙ Bread   ○ Wine   ○ Time

Date/Time of Offer	Amount Offered	Good Requested	Amount Requested
01/06/04 at 12:02 PM	6.00	Wine	2.00
01/06/04 at 4:41 PM	10.00	Time	4.00

You have 0.00 loaves of Bread, 0.00 bottles of Wine,
and 100.00 hours of Time to barter.

[Refresh List]   [Accept Offer]

If you receive time in a trade, you are hiring another player to help you produce a good. You have to click on one of the radio buttons below the offers list to indicate which good is to be produced with the time you are receiving.

Functions
The top table displays the utility and production functions for the group to which you belong. The functions of other groups are shown in the second table. Note that you do not need to actually use the functions to calculate anything because the program will do the calculations for you. The functions are displayed just for your information.

Graphs
This section provides you with important information about what other players in the game are doing. Select the graph you want to view from the dropdown menu. The menu options are described below.

- *Production by Period* Displays the total amount produced of each good by period.
- *Consumption by Period* Displays the total amount consumed of each good by period.
- *Current Stocks* Displays the total amount of each good currently held in stock.

- *Utility with Current Stocks, My Group* Displays the current utility values for each player in your attribute group.
- *Utility, All Periods, My Group* Displays the utility values for each player in your attribute group. The utility displayed is the sum of your current utility and your utility from all previous periods. At the end of the game your performance is evaluated based on your total utility from all periods relative to the total utility of the other students in your group.
- *Utility, All Periods, by Group* The graph displays a two-tone bar graph for each user group. The bars represent the sum of the utilities from previous periods and the current period. The height of the bar represents the maximum utility value for that group; the height of the dividing line between the two colors represents the median value (the middle value for people in that group).
- *Exchange Rate* Separate graphs are available for each of the three possible pairs of goods. The graphs display the exchange rates for the last 20 accepted offers. The exchange rate is the amount of one good that had to be given up to get one unit of another good. For example, assume someone traded 20 units of wine for 10 units of bread. The exchange rate of wine for bread in that trade would be 2, because two units of wine were traded away for each unit of bread received. You need to pay attention to the order in which the goods are listed. The numerical value of the exchange rate tells you how many units of the first good had to be given up to get one unit of the second good mentioned.

Record

This page presents a summary of your transactions by period under the **Inventory** table (see Figure 17). The **Utility Calculation** portion shows what your utility would be if you consumed all of your current stock of bread, wine and leisure (or how your utility was calculated if you are viewing the Record for a period that is already completed).

Figure 17: The Record

Record for Kevin Stanek in Period: 1

Inventory

Transaction	Date/Time	Bread	Wine	Leisure
Initial values		0.00	0.00	100.00
Produced Bread	12/29/03 at 3:10 PM	13.20		4.00
Produced Wine			30.31	4.00
Current Inventory		13.20	30.31	92.00

Utility Calculation

Utility If All Stock Consumed (Group 1) $= (Bread^{0.5})(Wine^{0.2})(Leisure^{0.2})$
$= ((13.20)^{0.5})((30.31)^{0.2})(92.00^{0.2})$
$= 17.76$

LEARNING ACTIVITIES & EXERCISES

The purpose of these exercises is to illustrate the principles you are learning in class using Jeremy's Market. The exercises are organized into five topic areas: Production, Consumption, Opportunity Cost, Production and Consumption in a Robinson Crusoe economy (Jeremy's Island) and Production and Consumption in a barter economy. Each topic begins with a brief discussion of the relevant concepts and their theoretical basis, and is followed by a set of activities that demonstrate how to use the concepts while participating in the game.

1. Production

OVERVIEW

Economists define production as using inputs, (like labor and raw materials), to produce output (like food and clothing) using the available technology. This section examines some basic concepts about production, including: production functions, marginal product, and the law of diminishing marginal returns.

1.2. PRODUCTION FUNCTIONS

Theory
In Jeremy's Market you spend time to produce goods. One important issue is how many units of a good you could make with some amount of time. For example, if you were producing bread, how many loaves could you make if you spent 10 hours producing bread?

The answer to that question will depend on what kind of equipment you have to work with and your knowledge in baking. Economists represent the relationship between the amount of time spent and the output produced with a mathematical formula called a production function. The function is designed to include all the factors that determine the level of output. Economists frequently assume that some inputs cannot be changed. The amount produced will then depend on how many units of the variable inputs (inputs that can be changed) are used. For example, if labor is the only variable input, the level of output (Q) will vary directly with the number of hours spent producing the good. The general form of the production function can then be written as:

$$Q = f(Hours) \tag{1}$$

The specific form of the function will depend on the level of technology and the amount of available equipment. A very simple production function might look something like this:

$$\text{Bread} = 10(\text{Hours}^{.5}) \tag{2}$$

Since the number of hours for making bread can be varied, we can pick different amounts of time and see how many loaves will be produced. For example, if we spent 9 hours making bread, 30 loaves would be produced. That is:

$$\text{Bread} = 10(9^{0.5}) = 10(3) = 30 \tag{3}$$

In the production function above the exponent on hours of labor was 0.5, which is the same as taking the square root. How could we calculate the amount produced if the exponent were a number other than 0.5? Most calculators can easily solve this type of problem for you. On your calculator, look for a button labeled "y^x." For example, to find the value of $9^{0.5}$ you would type "9," press "y^x," type ".5," and press "=." The answer "3" will be displayed. To show that $16^{.25}$ is equal to 2, perform similar operations: "16," "y^x," ".25," and "=".

Activities

Activity 1: Using Functions
Click on the Functions link and find the production functions for the two goods (bread and wine) that you produce. Which good do you think you are better at producing? Explain your answer.

Activity 2: Using a hand Calculator
Can you find the amount (Q) you will produce of each good with 30 hours of time using a calculator? Do the results match the numbers in the worksheet?

Activity 3: Production on Jeremy's Island
Select 40 hours for leisure time and spend 30 hours producing bread and 30 hours producing wine.
    A. Which good did you produce more of? Did that seem consistent with the functions listed in the ticker area?
    B. Were the amounts produced consistent with the value you calculated in Activity 2?

Activity 3: Production on Jeremy's Island
Use the information in columns 2 and 3 of Figure 18 to answer these questions. Assume you have these production functions:

$\text{Bread} = 10(\text{Hours}^{0.2})$
$\text{Wine} = 10(\text{Hours}^{0.8})$

A. How many hours were used for leisure?

B. How many units of each good were produced?

Figure 18: Production and Utility Table

Production and Utility

	Hours Spent Producing	Units Produced	Output from Last Hour (MP)	Utility from Last Unit Consumed (MU)	Utility from Last Hour Producing This Good (MP)(MU)
Leisure	▬	▬	▬	▬	▬
Bread	4.25	▬	▬	▬	▬
Wine	80.75	▬	▬	▬	▬

Utility after consuming output: 23.52

Activity 5: Production Using the Worksheet

Suppose you want to produce additional units of bread and wine using 40 hours and 20 hours, respectively. How much more of each good would you produce?

1.3. MARGINAL PRODUCT

Theory

We frequently want to know how much output will be produced when one more unit of an input is used. Economists refer to the additional output produced as "Marginal Product" (MP). So the question to consider in deciding how to spend your labor time is how much additional output will be produced when you spend one more hour producing the good. This is called the marginal product of labor (MP). It is computed as the change in total output (Q) divided by the change in the number of hours spent producing the good.

The production function of equation 2 above [Bread $= 10(\text{Hours}^{0.5})$] was used to generate the total output of bread in the table below. The MP values in column 3 were then computed. For example, the change in labor from 2 to 3 is 1 (i.e., 3-2); the change in output from 14.1 to 17.3 is 3.2 (i.e., 17.3-14.1). Thus, when three hours of labor is used the MP = 3.2 (i.e., 3.2÷1).

Table 2

Hours of Labor	Loaves of Bread (Q)	Marginal Product (MPL)
1	10	–
2	14.1	4.1
3	17.3	3.2

Activities

Activity 1: Using a Hand Calculator
Consider Table 2. If the fourth hour of labor is used to make bread,
  A. how many loaves will be produced?
  B. what will the marginal product be?

Activity 2: Using Jeremy's Island
This activity assumes that you are stranded on Jeremy's Island. Set the number of hours of leisure to 80 in the **Possible Production Combinations** table.
  A. From the **Production and Utility** table, how many units of bread would you produce in nine hours? Increase the amount of labor used to 10 hours. What is the marginal product of the tenth hour?
  B. Change the number of hours spent producing bread from 10 to 11. How many units of bread would be produced? What is the marginal product of the eleventh hour?
  C. **Advanced.** Calculus can be used to find the value of MP at a specific point. Explain how calculating MP using calculus would be different from finding MP using two points.

Activity 3: Using the Worksheet
  A. Suppose you want to produce additional bread and wine using 40 hours and 30 hours, respectively. How much of each good will you produce?
  B. Now, increase the number hours for producing bread to 41, while keeping your labor time for producing wine 30 hours. What is the marginal product of bread? What is the marginal product of wine? Please explain your answer.

1.4. THE LAW OF DIMINISHING MARGINAL RETURNS

Theory
This Law of Diminishing Marginal Returns applies to production when some inputs remain fixed while others vary. As more units of a variable input are combined with fixed inputs, the marginal product of the variable input will ultimately decline. The reason for this is that the ratio of the number of units of the variable input to the number of units of the fixed input is changing. For example, think of hiring additional employees to work in a factory. Since there is a limited amount of equipment for the employees to work with, at some point the increase in output from hiring an additional employee will be lower than the increase in output from the previous employee.

Table 2 provided an example of the law of diminishing returns. When the second hour of time was used to produce bread 4.1 additional loaves were produced, but only 3.2 loaves were produced when the third hour of labor was added.

Activities

Activity 1: Validating the Law of Diminishing Marginal Returns using the Worksheet
In this activity, you will keep leisure fixed while you vary the labor time for producing bread from zero to six. You will then record your hours worked and total output (Q) in Table 3.

Table 3

Hours	Total Output (Q)	MP
0		
1		
2		
3		
4		
5		
6		

    A.   At what level of output did the Law of Diminishing Marginal Returns begin?
    B.   What was the corresponding level of employment?
    C.   Do the reported MP_L values validate or invalidate the law of Diminishing Marginal Returns? Write a brief report based on your findings.

Activity 2: Using a Hand Calculator
Suppose the production function for bread was Bread = 10(Hours of Labor). Would it be consistent with the Law of Diminishing Marginal Returns? Why or why not? Please explain.

1.5. OPPORTUNITY COST

Theory
The opportunity cost of something is the value of the next best alternative that was foregone. Opportunity costs exist because resources are scarce; we can't produce infinite amounts of all goods. In Jeremy's Market the most scarce resource is time; your household has a limited number of hours that can be used to produce bread, produce wine, and consume as leisure time. To produce more of one thing resources must be shifted away from producing something else. This implies that in Jeremy's Market the opportunity cost of producing more units of bread could be measured in terms of the units of wine that must be sacrificed to produce the additional bread.

Typically, the opportunity cost of a good will increase as more units of that good are produced. Economists refer to this phenomenon as the Law of Increasing Opportunity Cost. Table 4 provides an example of increasing opportunity cost. When the first ten units of bread are produced, the opportunity cost is 5 units of wine, because wine production falls from 100 to 95. For the next ten units of bread, the opportunity cost is 10 units of wine, since production falls from 95 to 85. As more bread is produced the amount of wine sacrificed keeps rising.

Table 4

Possible Combination	Wine	Bread
A	100	0
B	95	10
C	85	20
D	70	30
E	40	40
F	0	50

Economists frequently use a graph called a production possibilities frontier to represent the concepts of opportunity cost and increasing opportunity cost.

For example, if we graphed the values in the table above we would have a production possibilities frontier as shown in Figure 19.

Figure 19: Production Possibilities Frontier

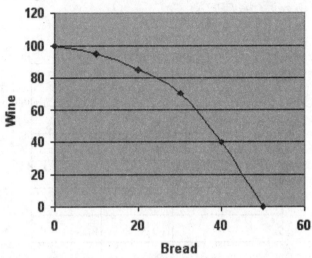

The concept of opportunity cost is illustrated by the PPF because as you move to points with greater consumption of bread, you have to reduce the amount of wine consumed. We can also think of the slope of the PPF as representing the size of the opportunity cost. For example, assume we move from consuming 10 units of bread and 95 units of wine to 20 units of bread and 85 units of wine. The slope of the PPF between those two points would be -1 [(95-85)/(10-20) = (10)/(-10) = -1], which indicates that for each additional unit of bread you consume you must give up a unit of wine.

On the other hand, if we move from consuming 20 units of bread and 85 units of wine to 30 units of bread and 70 units of wine, the slope of the PPF between those points is -1.5 [(85-70/(20-30) = (15)/(-10) = -1.5]. The increase in the opportunity cost is represented by the slope of the PPF growing steeper as more bread is consumed. This gives the PPF its bowed out (or concave) shape.

Activities
Activity 1: Drawing the PPF

Table 5

Possible Combination	Wine	Bread
A	260	0
B	250	10
C	225	20
D	175	30
E	100	40
F	0	50

A. Use the data in Table 5 to draw a graph of the PPF and label all the possible combinations. Hint: Put Wine on the vertical axis and Bread on the horizontal axis.
B. Can this economy produce 30 units of bread and 200 units of wine? Why or Why not?
C. Can this economy produce 20 units of bread and 100 units of wine? What would it imply if it did?

Activity 2: Evaluating opportunity cost using the slope of the PPF
A. Calculate the slopes of the PPF between B and C, and between D and E.
B. Between B and C, what is the opportunity cost of producing one more unit of bread?
C. Between D and E, what is the opportunity cost of producing one more unit of bread?

Activity 3: Representing increasing opportunity costs using the slope of the PPF
A. Moving from A to F, are the absolute values of the slope increasing or decreasing? Please explain.
B. Moving from A to F, is the opportunity cost of production an additional unit of bread increasing or decreasing? Please explain.
C. **Advanced.** Assume the production functions for bread and wine were as follows:

$$Bread = 10(Hours) \qquad Wine = 10(Hours)$$

How would the shape of the PPF differ from the PPF in Figure 19? What would it imply about opportunity costs?

2. Consumption

OVERVIEW

Every consumer has a goal: To maximize his or her total utility from all the goods and services that he or she can afford to buy. Total utility represents the level of happiness that is derived by consuming some combination of goods and services. The relationship between the level of happiness and the amount of each good or service consumed is called the utility function. The contribution to the total happiness (or utility) by consuming one more unit of the good or service is called marginal utility.

Since consumers' preferences differ, the combination of goods they will select will differ. Consumers will also choose different combinations of goods because their incomes differ. However, all consumers must pay the same prices for the same products or services.

We can analyze consumers' choices either in terms of marginal utility (MU) or in terms of the marginal rate of substitution (MRS). If your instructor is discussing consumer choice in terms of MU, you should read sections 2.1, 2.2, and 2.3. If your instructor is discussing consumer choice in terms of MRS, you should look at sections 2.1, 2.4, and 2.5.

2.1. UTILITY FUNCTIONS

Theory
In the production section we focused on the relationship between one input (labor hours) and output (bread or wine). The relationship between total utility (U) and the quantity consumed of the different goods can also be represented with a mathematical function. For example, the general form of a utility function where a consumer gains utility from consuming bread, wine, and leisure time can be stated as:

$$U = f(\text{Bread, Wine, Leisure Time}) \qquad (1)$$

All else remaining constant, the greater the number of units consumed of each good, the higher the level of total utility. Your utility is determined by the utility function assigned to your attribute group. A typical utility function would look like this:

$$U = 10\,[(\text{Bread}^{0.5})\,(\text{Wine}^{0.3})\,(\text{Leisure Time}^{0.2})] \qquad (2)$$

If you click the **Functions** link, your household's utility function will be displayed under **Utility and Production Functions for Your Group**.

As an illustration, suppose that you have 100 hours to spend towards producing bread and wine, or enjoying as leisure time. Let's assume you chose to allocate the 100 hours in as follows: 1 hour for bread production, 19 hours for wine production, and 80 hours for leisure. If the corresponding total output for each good is 10 units of bread, 18.02 units of wine and 80 units of leisure time, then as a consumer, your total utility from consuming this amount of each good can be computed as:

$$U = 10^{0.5} \times 18.02^{0.3} \times 80^{0.2} \qquad (3)$$
$$= 3.162 \times 2.381 \times 2.402$$
$$= 18.08$$

This is the level of utility (or the amount of satisfaction measured in utils) that you have derived by consuming the combination of 10 units of bread, 18.02 units of wine, and 80 units of leisure time. The ticker displays the utility you would have by consuming the goods and leisure time you have in stock.

Activities

Activity 1: Using the Functions
Click on the **Functions** link to display your utility function.
    A. Write down the utility function.
    B. Which good appears to contribute the most to your total utility? Please explain.
    C. Which good appears to contribute the least to your total utility? Please explain
    D. If you did not consume any of the goods, what would your utility be?

Activity 2: Using Jeremy's Island and a hand Calculator
From the dropdown list, choose to spend 30 hours producing bread and 30 hours producing wine, leaving 40 hours for leisure. From the *Production and Utility* table:
    A. How many units of each good would you produce?
    B. What is the total utility that you derive by consuming them?
    C. Using a hand calculator and the consumption function that you wrote down in Activity 1, show that the reported total utility is correct.

Activity 3: Reading the Production and Utility Table on Jeremy's Island
Suppose you spend 5 hours producing each good.
    A. What is your utility with this combination?
    B. Now decrease the number of hours of leisure to 80 by choosing to spend 10 hours producing each good. Did your utility rise? Explain why your utility changed. Do you think you could increase your utility

further?

Activity 4: Reading the Utility Calculations Table of the Worksheet
Suppose you spend additional 40 hours to produce bread and 20 hours to
produce wine. Are you better off or worse off in terms of the amount of utility
achieved?

2.2. MARGINAL UTILITY

(Skip to 2.4 if your instructor is discussing consumer choice in terms of MRS)

Theory
Marginal utility (MU) is the change in total utility that occurs when one more
unit of a good is consumed while leaving the consumption of all other goods the
same. For example, Table 6 shows possible bundles of bread (B), wine (W) and
leisure time (T) and their total utility. The utility values are derived from the
function:

$$U = 10 [(Bread^{0.2}) (Wine^{0.2}) (Lesiure\ Time^{0.4})] \qquad (4)$$

The amount of bread consumed increased from 10 loaves to 11 loaves,
increasing utility from 11.9 to 12.3 and the corresponding MU is 0.4 (12.3 -
11.9). This means that the additional utility from consuming the last loaf of
bread (marginal utility of the last loaf) was 0.4 utils. MU thus allows us to
measure how much your well being has increased by consuming one more loaf
of one good versus another. For example, if the MU of bread is 1, and the MU
of wine is 2, consuming one more unit of wine will yield more utility than
consuming another loaf of bread.

Table 6

Bread	Wine	Leisure Time	Utility	Marginal Utility (MU)
10	15	40	11.9	—
11	15	40	12.3	0.4
12	15	40	12.4	0.3
13	15	40	12.6	
14	15	40		0.1

Activities

Activity 1: Calculating Marginal Utilities
A. In the table above, calculate the value for marginal utility when the individual is consuming 13 units of bread.
B. Given the value of MU when 14 units of bread are consumed, what is the value of total utility?

Activity 2: Interpreting Marginal Utilities
A. Assume the marginal utility of bread is 3 and the marginal utility of leisure is 1. If it took one hour to produce an additional unit of bread, would you be better off spending the next hour producing bread or enjoying the hour as leisure time?
B. b. Assume the marginal utility of bread and wine are the same. If it took the same amount of time to produce another unit of bread as one more unit of wine, would you be better off spending the next hour producing bread or wine?
C. If the MU of bread was zero, what would that imply about how your utility would change with the consumption of another unit of bread?

Activity 3: Reading the Production and Utility Table on Jeremy's Island.
The following questions refer to Figure 20.
A. By how much does an additional hour of leisure add to total utility?
B. By how much does an additional unit of bread add to total utility?
C. By how much does an additional unit of wine add to total utility?

Figure 20: Production and Utility Table (Jeremy's Island)

Production and Utility

	Hours Spent Producing	Units Produced	Output from Last Hour (MP)	Utility from Last Unit Consumed (MU)	Utility from Last Hour Producing This Good (MP)(MU)
Leisure	40.00	40.00	1.00	0.25	0.25
Bread	21.00	33.80	0.64	0.30	0.19
Wine	39.00	90.08	1.39	0.11	0.15

Utility after consuming output: 33.55

Activity 4: Reading the Utility Calculations Table of the Worksheet
A. Suppose you produce additional bread and wine using 40 hours and 30 hours, respectively. How much is your current level of utility?

B.   Now, increase the number hours for producing bread to 41 hours while keeping the number of hours for producing wine at 30 hours. How much is your current level of utility? Did your utility rise or fall? Explain why it could have changed in either direction.

2.3. THE LAW OF DIMINISHING MARGINAL UTILITY

Theory
The law of diminishing marginal utility says that as more units of a good are consumed, marginal utility will fall, if all else is held constant. For example, assume you are very thirsty and you drink a glass of water. You are now much more comfortable, so drinking the glass of water caused a substantial increase in your utility. If you drink a second glass of water your utility will still go up (let's assume you were a little thirsty), but the increase in your utility from the second glass will not be nearly as large as the increase from the first glass. Refer to the example in table 2 once again and examine the marginal utility (MU) values in the last column. The decrease in MU as more units of bread are consumed illustrates this law.

Activities

Activity 1: Exploring the Law of Diminishing Marginal Utility
A.   Is Table 6 in the previous section consistent with the Law of Diminishing Marginal Utility?
B.   Assume a consumer had the following utility function:
     U = Bread + Wine
     Would that function be consistent with the law of diminishing marginal utility? Explain why or why not.

Activity 2: Validating the Law of Diminishing Marginal Utility using a Hand Calculator
Consider the illustrative example above and the utility function:
$$U = 10 [(Bread^{0.2}) (Wine^{0.2}) (Leisure\ Time^{0.5})].$$
Assume that this person is consuming 10 units of bread, 10 units of wine, and 64 hours of leisure.
A.   Find the consumer's level of utility.
B.   If the individual consumes another unit of bread, what will his or her utility be? What was the marginal utility of the 11th unit of bread?
C.   Now assume the individual consumes a 12th unit of bread. Is the marginal utility of the 12th unit lower than the 11th unit?

D. Are the results in sections A to C consistent with the Law of Diminishing Marginal Utility? Explain your answer.

Activity 3: Validating the Law of Diminishing Marginal Utility using the Worksheet
Marginal utility is measured by changing the amount consumed of one good while holding everything else constant. Can you properly estimate marginal utility by varying the amount of time you spend producing bread and looking at the change in utility? Hint: Is the consumption of all other goods remaining the same?

2.4. MARGINAL RATE OF SUBSTITUTION

(If your instructor is covering consumer choice in terms of MU, skip sections 2.4 and 2.5)

Theory
The marginal rate of substitution represents the tradeoff that a consumer is willing to make between two goods while holding utility constant. For example, if the marginal rate of substitution of wine for bread is 5, that implies that the consumer feels that the last unit of bread consumed gives him as much utility as the last 5 units of wine.

The MRS can help us predict how the consumer will respond to different opportunities. For example, if the consumer's MRS was 5 and if it were possible for the consumer to get more bread by giving up 3 units of wine, then the consumer would want to acquire additional bread. In that case the consumer would be better off because he or she is giving up 3 units of wine for something that had a value of 5 units of wine.

Graphically, the MRS is represented by the slope of an indifference curve. An indifference curve represents all of the different combinations of two goods that give the consumer the same level of happiness.

Activities

Activity 1: Exploring MRS

Figure 21: Tradeoffs in Production and MRS

	Tradeoff in Production	MRS
Wine Units for 1 Bread Unit	2.32	2.32
Bread Units for 1 Hour of Time	0.66	0.66
Wine Units for 1 Hour of Time	1.54	1.54

A. Given the information shown in Figure 21, how many units of bread is the last hour of leisure time worth to this consumer?
B. If this consumer were given an offer to trade 12 units of bread for 1 unit of leisure, would he or she want to make that trade? Explain your answer.

Activity 2: Calculating MRS

A. If the consumer's utility function is: $U = (Bread^{0.5})(Wine^{0.5})$ and the formula for the MRS is: MRS = Wine/Bread, what will the consumer's MRS equal if he or she is consuming 16 units of bread and 1 unit of wine?
B. What would the slope of the indifference curve be at that combination of bread and wine?

2.5. DECLINING MARGINAL RATE OF SUBSTITUTION

Theory
Economists typically assume that as a person consumes more of a good the last unit consumed of that good is considered less valuable than the previous units. For example, if you only had access to one loaf of bread per week, that loaf would be very valuable to you. On the other hand, if you had access to 100 loaves of bread per week, the value of the last loaf would be much lower.

As discussed in the previous section, the MRS represents the value to the consumer of the last unit consumed in terms of some other good. If, as we consume more of a good (while holding utility constant), the last unit consumed becomes less valuable to us we would expect the MRS to decline. In other words, we would expect the MRS of wine for bread to be higher when we only have one loaf of bread than when we have 100 loaves.

Graphically, the MRS is represented by the absolute value of the slope of the indifference curve. When the consumer is consuming very little of the good on the X axis, we would expect MRS to be very high and the slope to be very steep. When the consumer is consuming a large amount of the good on the X-axis, the MRS should be lower and the slope of the indifference curve will be relatively flat. As a result, we expect the indifference curve to be bowed away from the origin (the 0, 0 point on the graph).

Activities

Activity 1: Exploring Declining MRS
Table 7 is based on the utility function: $U = (Bread^{0.5})(Wine^{0.5})$, so the formula for MRS would be: MRS = Wine/Bread.

Table 7

Bread	Wine	Utility	MRS
1	16	4	16
4	4	4	1
16	1	4	0.0625

A. Given the table above, explain how the values are consistent with the assumption of a declining MRS.
B. If the consumer had consumed 0.25 units of bread, how much wine would he or she need to consume (holding utility constant at 4) and what would the MRS be? Is that result consistent with the assumption of a declining MRS?

Figure 22: PPF and Indifference Curve

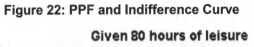

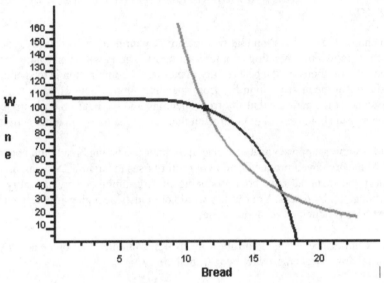

A. Given the graph shown in Figure 22, compare the absolute value of the slope of the indifference curve when the individual is consuming 10 units of bread and when she is consuming 20 units. Is this consistent with the assumption of declining MRS? Explain your answer.

B. If the indifference curve were a straight line, would that be consistent with the assumption of declining MRS? Explain your answer.

3. Production and Consumption in a Robinson Crusoe Economy (Jeremy's Island)

OVERVIEW

In a Robinson Crusoe economy there is no trade; households only produce output for their own consumption. Your goal is to use your household's time to produce and consume the best possible combination of goods and leisure.

There are two ways to discuss the utility-maximizing choice, either in terms of marginal utility or in terms of the marginal rate of substitution. If your instructor is discussing consumer choice in terms of MU, go to section 4.1. If your instructor is discussing consumer choice in terms of MRS, skip to section 4.2.

3.1. CONSUMPTION AND PRODUCTION WITHOUT TRADE IN TERMS OF MU

To choose the combination that will maximize your household's utility, you need to know how spending another hour on each good will alter your utility. The rule for choosing the best (utility maximizing) combination is to spend your time so that the increase in utility from spending another hour on each activity is the same. If the additional utility from spending another hour on one activity is higher, you should spend more time on that activity and less on other activities.

For example, suppose you spend one more hour producing bread, you consume all of the bread you produced, and your utility rises by 10 utils. Now assume that if you spent the same hour producing and consuming wine your utility would go up by 6 utils. Your utility would obviously be higher if you spent the next hour producing bread than wine.

You can find the change in utility from spending another hour on an activity by multiplying marginal product by marginal utility.

$$(MP)(MU) = \left(\frac{\Delta U}{\Delta Q}\right)\left(\frac{\Delta Q}{\Delta H}\right) = \frac{\Delta U}{\Delta H}$$

The best combination to produce and consume is achieved when the utility gained from the last hour spent in producing and consuming wine, bread, and leisure are all equal. That is:

$$(MP_{Wine})(MU_{Wine}) = (MP_{Bread})(MU_{Bread}) = (MP_{Leisure})(MU_{Leisure})$$

If $(MP_{Wine})(MU_{Wine}) > (MP_{Bread})(MU_{Bread})$ you should re-allocate more time to wine production and less time to bread production in order to maximize your total utility from wine, bread and leisure. On the other hand, if $(MP_{Wine})(MU_{Wine}) < (MP_{Bread})(MU_{Bread})$ you should devote more time to bread production. Note that the $MP_{Leisure}$ is always unit (1) since one hour of time always produces one hour of leisure. The values for (MP)(MU) are listed in the right-hand column of the Production and Utility table.

Activities
The following activities refer to Jeremy's Island with Robinson Crusoe as the only resident.

Activity 1: Choosing the Utility Maximizing Output Combination
Use Figure 23 to answer the following questions:

Figure 23: Production and Utility Table

Production and Utility

	Hours Spent Producing	Units Produced	Output from Last Hour (MP)	Utility from Last Unit Consumed (MU)	Utility from Last Hour Producing This Good (MP)(MU)
Leisure	30.00	30.00	1.00	0.29	▇
Bread	56.00	50.04	0.36	0.17	▇
Wine	14.00	48.72	2.09	0.18	▇

Utility after consuming output: 28.79

A. How much utility is gained from the last hours spent on producing and consuming leisure, bread, and wine?
B. Based on your results in part A above, should Robinson Crusoe reallocate his time in order to maximize his utility? Why or why not?
C. Why would you be unable to leave Jeremy's Island when you click on the "Check Answer" button?

Activity 2: Using the Possible Production Combinations and Production and Utility Table to Search for the Utility Maximizing Outputs
Suppose Robinson Crusoe chooses to spend 85 hours for leisure, 12 hours for bread production, and 3 hours for wine production. Use the worksheet to do the following:

A. What is the marginal product of i) leisure, ii) bread, and iii) wine?
B. What is the marginal utility of i) leisure, ii) bread, and iii) wine?
C. How much utility does he gain from the last hour spent on producing and consuming i) leisure, ii) bread, and iii) wine?
D. From part C above, is the utility gained from the last hour spent in producing and consuming bread, wine and leisure the same? If not how should he re-allocate his resource (time) between the three activities in order to increase his total utility?
E. Find the best combination of bread, wine, and leisure that will give Robinson Crusoe the highest utility. Write a brief report of your findings.

3.2. CONSUMPTION AND PRODUCTION WITHOUT TRADE IN TERMS OF MRS

As noted earlier, MRS represents the value of the last unit consumed of one good in terms of the number of units of another good. For example, if the MRS of wine for bread is 5, this implies that the last unit of bread is worth 5 units of wine.

Given an MRS of wine for bread of 5, if the consumer can get more than 5 units of wine by giving up the last unit of bread he or she will be better off. On the other hand, if the consumer could give up 2 units of wine and get a unit of bread, then the consumer would be better off consuming more bread. So the key is to compare the value the consumer puts on the last unit of bread with the possible tradeoff in bread and wine.

When there is no trade, the amount of additional wine the consumer must give up to get another unit of bread is determined by the production functions. As discussed earlier in the section on opportunity cost, the number of units of wine that must be given up is the opportunity cost of the next unit of bread. Graphically, the opportunity cost is represented by the slope of the production possibilities frontier.

The consumer will have maximized his or her utility when the MRS equals the opportunity cost, because there will be no incentive to make additional changes in production or consumption.

Activities

Activity 1: Choosing the Utility Maximizing Output Combination
Use Figure 24 to answer the following questions:

Figure 24: Tradeoff in Production and MRS

	Tradeoff in Production	MRS
Wine Units for 1 Bread Unit	2.32	2.32
Bread Units for 1 Hour of Time	0.66	0.66
Wine Units for 1 Hour of Time	1.54	1.54

    A.   In terms of wine, what value does this person put on the last unit of bread? What is the opportunity cost of the last unit of bread?

B. Is this individual consuming the optimal combination of bread and wine? Explain your answer.

Activity 2: Choosing the Utility Maximizing Combination Graphically
Use Figure 25 to answer the following questions:

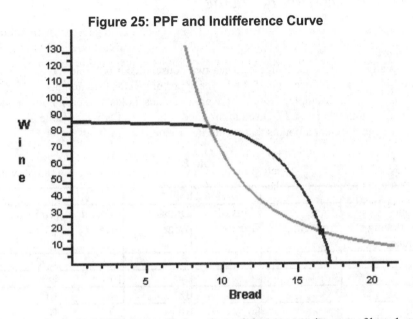

Figure 25: PPF and Indifference Curve

A. Does the MRS of wine for bread equal the opportunity cost of bread at the point marked by the black box? Explain how you came up with your answer.
B. Should the consumer produce more bread and less wine or less bread and more wine in this case?
C. Draw a picture showing a situation where the consumer has maximized his or her utility.

4. Production and Consumption in a Barter (or an Exchange) Economy

OVERVIEW

In reality, no economy can be characterized as self-sufficient. Economists use the Robinson Crusoe model as a standard for measuring the potential gains from trade. Gains from trade occur because different individuals (or nations) have different opportunity costs in producing a good. Individuals and nations that specialize in those productive activities for which they have a smaller opportunity cost are said to have comparative advantage and can reap significant benefits by trading.

4.1. SPECIALIZATION AND TRADE

Theory
Mutually beneficial exchange between two households is possible if one household can produce a good at a lower opportunity cost than another household. For example, assume there are two households, and each household has four hours that could be used to produce either bread or wine. Table 8 shows the different amounts that would be produced by the households.

Table 8

Hours Producing Bread	Hours Producing Wine	Household A		Household B	
		Units of Bread	Units of Wine	Units of Bread	Units of Wine
0	4	0	28	0	100
1	3	40	24	10	90
2	2	70	18	18	70
3	1	90	10	24	40
4	0	100	0	28	0

Suppose initially both households spent two hours producing bread and two hours producing wine. In this case the total amount of bread produced would be 88 (70 units by household A and 18 by household B), and the total amount of wine produced would also be 88.

If Household A spends another hour in bread production, it can make 20 more units of bread at the cost of an 8 unit reduction in the output of wine, so on average the household would only sacrifice 0.4 units of wine for each unit of bread. On the other hand, if household B were to spend another hour producing bread, it would only gain 6 additional units of bread, and would sacrifice 30 units of wine, a loss of 5 units of wine for each unit of bread.

Since the opportunity cost of producing bread is lower for household A, that household has a comparative advantage in bread production. We can use the same argument to show that B has a comparative advantage in wine production.

Now suppose both households specialize in producing the good where their opportunity cost is lower. The total output of both bread and wine would rise to 200 units. If the households trade, it is then possible for both households to consume more of both goods than they did when trade was not possible.

To maximize your utility in the game you first need to identify the good that you have a comparative advantage in producing. The **Functions** page displays the functions for all of the attribute groups. In a typical game you will have a comparative advantage in the good you can produce the most of in one hour. You then want to specialize in the production of that good, and trade for the good in which you do not have a comparative advantage. When trading, you should also seek to trade at an exchange rate that maximizes the amount received in trade.

MarketSim lists the exchange rates for the most recently accepted trades. The exchange rate, the rate at which one good is traded for another, is useful in deciding whether you should try to get more of a good by producing it yourself or trading for it. For example, suppose you want to consume more bread, and your production function for bread is: $B=10Hours^{0.2}$. If you spend five hours producing bread you will make 13.8 units of bread. Also assume your production function for wine is: $W=10Hours^{0.8}$, with 5 hours of time you would produce 36.2 units of wine.

Your next step is to try to trade wine for bread. Table 9 shows three different offers and the associated exchange rates. In case of the first offer, you would actually have less bread by trading than if you simply produced bread.

The next two offers show that you are clearly much better off by producing and trading wine since you will end up 36 units of wine and 72 loaves of bread, respectively. Note however that the exchange rate of wine for bread will depend on the offers that other participants in the game are willing to accept.

Table 9

Offer	Wine (W)	Bread	Exchange Rate: Wine for Bread
1	36	9	4
2	36	36	1
3	36	72	0.5

Activities

Activity 1: Validating the Principle of Specialization and Exchange
Suppose two individuals (1 and 2) produce bread (B) and Wine (W) using the
following production functions:

$$\text{Household 1: } B = 10(\text{Hours}^{0.4}) \qquad W = 10(\text{Hours}^{0.8})$$
$$\text{Household 2: } B = 10(\text{Hours}^{0.8}) \qquad W = 10(\text{Hours}^{0.4})$$

A. Which household has a comparative advantage in the production of
bread? Of wine? Explain how you came to your answers.
B. Fill in the blank cells in both parts of Table 10. Show that the total
amount produced of both goods was higher when the households
specialized.

Table 10

Section A, No Specialization

Household	Good	Hours	Output
1	Bread	5	
	Wine	5	
2	Bread	5	
	Wine	5	

Section B, Specialization

Household	Good	Hours	Output
1	Bread	0	
	Wine	10	
2	Bread	10	
	Wine	0	

A. Consider Section A above. If the exchange rate is one unit of wine for
one unit of bread, how much more will each household get to
consume when there is specialization and trade, as opposed to when
they both spend 5 hours producing each good?
B. Consider Section B above. If the exchange rate for trading bread and
wine were 100 units of wine for 1 unit of bread, would Household 1
still consume more of both goods with specialization?

Activity 2: Evaluating Gains from Trade using the Worksheet
A. Explain what the exchange rate tells us.
B. Assume you spend 30 hours producing bread, and 30 hours producing
wine. How much is produced of each good?

C. Let's call the good you made more of good A, and the good you made less of good B. How much of A and B would be produced if you spend 50 hours producing good A and 10 hours producing good B?

D. Given the output from part C, if you could trade 1 unit of good A for one unit of good B, would you be able to consume more than you did when you spent 30 hours producing each good? Will you be better off?

4.2. THE BARTER ECONOMY AND THE UTILITY-MAXIMIZING RULE (MUX/PX = MUY/PY)

(If your instructor is discussing consumer choice in terms of MU, skip to section 5.3)

Theory

The utility-maximizing rule states that consumers maximize their utility by picking combinations of goods such that the marginal utility per dollar is the same for all goods. The rule is frequently written as:

$$MUx/Px = MUy/Py$$

If MUx/Px is greater than MUy/Py, this means that you are getting more utility from the last dollar spent on X than the last dollar spent on Y, and you should purchase more X. As you buy more X the marginal utility of X will fall, as you buy less Y the marginal utility of Y will rise, and you will move towards meeting the utility-maximizing rule.

In Jeremy's Market all exchanges take place through barter. Since no money is used, there are no explicit prices. However, we can come up with implicit prices based on the exchange rates of the trades and use the utility-maximizing rule.

In Jeremy's Market the price of an hour of time is set at \$1. We can then calculate the prices for other goods relative to the price of labor. For example, assume that the exchange rate of bread for time was two units of bread for one hour of time. This implies that the value of a unit of bread is half the value of an hour of time, so the price of one unit of bread should be \$0.5, or 50 cents.

When you click on **Show** the table under the Utility Maximization section of the worksheet, you will need to type in values for the exchange rates. Using those values, the software will calculate the implicit prices of bread and wine and the values for MU/P of bread, wine, and leisure.

Activities

Activity 1: The Utility-Maximizing Rule

Table 11 shows the different combinations of two goods a household can consume with $10 (the price of X is $1 and the price of Y is $2). Fill in the empty cells in the table. If the household is consuming combination A, is it getting more utility from a dollar spent on X or a dollar spent on Y?

Table 11

Bundle	Units X	Mux	MUx/Px	Units Y	MUy	MUy/Py
A	1	14		4.5	22	
B	2	12		4	24	
C	3	10		3.5	26	

    A. Which bundle of the two goods maximizes the household's utility?
    B. Determine the Y-intercept and the X-intercept?
    C. Plot the budget line and locate the combinations represented by A, B, and C.

Activity 2: The Utility-Maximizing Rule and the Worksheet

Figure 26: Utility Maximization

Hide the table.

	Units Consumed	Exchange Rate (Units per hour)	Implicit Price	Marginal Utility	Marginal Utility per Dollar
Leisure	40.00	1.00	$1.00	7.74	7.74
Bread	76.96	3	$0.33	5.36	16.08
Wine	38.98	3	$0.33	7.94	23.81

    A. Given the values in Figure 26, what should the household consume more of? What should it consume less of? Explain your answer.
    B. What would the implicit price of bread be if the exchange rate was 10 units of bread for one hour of time? At that exchange rate, should the household consume more or less bread? Explain your logic.

Activity 3: The Utility-Maximizing Rule and the Worksheet

On the Worksheet, choose to spend 57 hours producing the good you are best at producing, 3 hours producing the other good, and leave 40 hours for leisure. In the **Consumption and Utility After Trades** section, assume the exchange rate of bread for one unit of time is 10, and the exchange rate of wine for one unit of time is 10.

    A. Which good(s) should you consume more of? Which good(s) should you consume less of? Be able to explain your logic.

    B. In the hypothetical trade section, trade 10 units of the good you want to consume less of for 10 units of the good you want to consume more of. Was the change in your utility consistent with the utility-maximizing rule?

4.3. THE BARTER ECONOMY AND THE UTILITY-MAXIMIZING RULE (MRS =PX/PY)

(If your instructor is discussing consumer choice in terms of MU you can skip this section)

Theory

The utility-maximizing rule states that consumers maximize their utility by picking combinations of goods such that the marginal rate of substitution equals the ratio of the prices of the two goods. The rule is frequently written as:

$$MRSxy = Px/Py$$

You can think of the marginal rate of substitution as the value of the last unit of X in terms of units of Y. For example, if we said that the marginal rate of substitution of wine for bread was 3, that implies that the consumer views the last unit of bread consumed as having the same value of three units of wine.

The ratio of the prices for the two goods represents the tradeoff between X and Y in the marketplace. For example, if the price of bread is $4 and the price of wine is $2, assuming that bread is X and wine is Y, the ratio of the prices would be 2. This implies that you would have to reduce your purchases of wine by two units to free up enough money to purchase one unit of bread.

If the MRS is greater than Px/Py, this implies that the value of the next unit of X, in terms of Y, is greater than the amount of Y the individual needs to give up to get another unit of X. For example if the MRS of wine for bread were 3 and the ratio of the prices was 2, this means that the consumer thinks the last unit of bread is worth three units of wine, but he or she only needs to give up 2 units of wine to get the next unit of bread. In this case he should buy more bread.

If the MRS is less than Px/Py, the value of the next unit of X, in terms of Y, is less than the amount of Y the individual would receive if he or she bought one fewer unit of X and spent the money on Y. For example, if the MRS of wine for bread were 3 and the ratio of the price of bread and wine were 5, this would mean that the person believes the last unit of bread is worth three units of wine, but if he or she reduces his or her consumption of bread by one unit he or she can buy 5 units of wine. Therefore, he or she should purchase more wine.

In Jeremy's Market all exchanges take place through barter. Since no money is used, there are no explicit prices. However, we can come up with implicit prices based on the exchange rates of the trades and use the utility-maximizing rule.

In Jeremy's Market the price of an hour of labor is set at $1. We can then calculate the prices for other goods relative to the price of labor. For example, assume that the exchange rate of bread for time was two units of bread for one hour of time. This implies that the value of a unit of bread is half the value of an hour of time, so the price of one unit of bread should be $0.5, or 50 cents.

In the section of the Worksheet page called **Consumption and Utility After Trade**, you will need to type in values for the exchange rates. Using those values, the software will calculate the implicit prices of bread and wine and the values for the price ratios. The Worksheet will also calculate the value for MRS using whatever combination of goods you specify.

Activities

Activity 1: The Utility-Maximizing Rule
Table 12 shows the different combinations of two goods a household can consume with $10 (the price of Bread is $1 and the price of Wine is $2).
   A. If the household is consuming combination A, what is the value of the last unit of bread in terms of wine?
   B. Given the ratio of the prices, how much bread could the household buy if it bought one less unit of wine?
   C. Would the household be better off if it moved from consuming bundle A to a combination with a little more bread and a little less wine? Explain your answer.
   D. Which bundle is consistent with the utility-maximizing rule? Explain your answer.

Table 12

Bundle	Units Bread	Units Wine	MRS
A	1	4.5	4
B	2	4	0.5
GC	3	3.5	0.1

Activity 2: The Utility-Maximizing Rule and the Worksheet

Figure 27: Utility Maximization

<u>Hide</u> the tables.

Units Consumed		MRS
Leisure	Wine Units for 1 Bread Unit	
	50.00	2.32
Bread	Bread Units for 1 Hour of Time	
	60.34	0.66
Wine	Wine Units for 1 Hour of Time	
	38.98	1.54

A. Given the values in Figure 27, if the exchange rate were 10 units of wine for one unit of bread, would this person want to consume more or less bread? Explain your answer.

B. What would the implicit price of bread be if the exchange rate were 10 units of bread for one hour of time (given 1 hour of time is worth $1)? At that exchange   rate, should the household consume more or less bread? Explain your logic.

Activity 3: The Utility-Maximizing Rule and the Worksheet
On the Worksheet, spend 57 hours producing the good you are best at producing, 3 hours producing the other good, and leave 40 hours for leisure. In the **Consumption and Utility after Trades** section, assume the exchange rate of bread for one unit of time is 10, and the exchange rate of wine for one unit of time is 10.

A. Which good(s) should you consume more of? Which good(s) should you consume less of? Be able to explain your logic.

B. In the hypothetical trade section, trade one hour of time for 10 units of bread. Was the change in your utility consistent with the utility-maximizing rule?

Adam's Market: A Monetary Economy

INTRODUCTION

Welcome to Adam's Market: A Monetary Economy. We hope you enjoy your experience. This Manual is designed to help you with questions you might have on the software. The Adam's Market section of this Manual is divided into four parts.

I.   The first part is this brief Introduction.

II. The second part gives an overview of the simulation, offers some tips on strategy, and gives brief descriptions of each component of an Adam's Market game. Much of this information is also available through the simulation's Help system.

III. The third part offers more details about each component of an Adam's Market Game.

IV. The fourth part presents a number of activities and exercises that relate Adam's Market to the economic theory you are learning in class. The activities are designed to help you better understand the key concepts of the circular flow model, utility maximization, labor supply, profit maximization in the short run, depreciation, profit maximization in the long run, entry and exit of firms, and the bond market.

OVERVIEW, STRATEGY TIPS, AND PROGRAM STRUCTURE

Overview

In Adam's Market you and your classmates are each responsible for both a consumer and a firm. Money is used to make transactions between firms and consumers. As a consumer, you need to decide how many hours you are going to work and what goods you will buy. As a firm, you need to decide how much labor time to hire and how much output to produce. In the more complex versions of the simulation, you will also need to decide whether to make additional investments in your firm's capital, whether to buy or sell bonds, and whether to change industries. Your goals are to try to maximize your consumer's happiness and the value of your firm.

The simulation is divided into periods. In each period of the simulation every consumer has use of some fixed number of hours (usually 100). You must sell those hours to earn income. Firms, in turn, buy the labor from consumers and then produce goods with the labor. At some point in the game, your professor might allow for the option to purchase capital. This usually occurs in later periods. The other decisions (bonds and entry/exit) are also optional and might or might not be included in your game.

Simulation Rules

Here are some important rules to help understand how Adam's Market works.

BOTH CONSUMERS AND FIRMS

- The game is divided into some number of periods chosen by your instructor.

- Any offers that have not been accepted at the end of a period expire and are removed from the list of available offers.

- Your grade will be determined by your participation and performance in the game. Performance is determined by the All Periods utility (current utility added to past utility from previous periods) of your consumer as well as the net worth (cash + value of inventory + value of capital stock + present discounted value of bonds) of your firm. Most likely your performance grade will be more heavily weighted on the performance of your consumer. Thus, it is in your best interest to transfer some money (dividends) from your firm to your consumer so that your consumer is able to reach a higher utility by spending more income. However, make sure you keep enough cash for your firm to purchase capital and labor. Also, since part of your grade is determined by firm net worth, you will not want to transfer all cash to the consumer.

Bond Market

- Your instructor has the option of enabling the bond market. If your instructor is not including the bond market in your game you may skip this "Bond Market" bulleted list.

- Bonds are a method of borrowing and lending money. If a firm sells a bond to a consumer or a different firm, the issuing firm is borrowing money from the bond buyer, and promising to pay some amount back at a future date. Firms might choose to borrow so they can make larger investments in capital.

- Only firms can issue new bonds (borrow money). Both firms and consumers can buy new bonds (lending money to the issuing firm). Bonds can be resold. For example, a consumer or firm could purchase a newly issued bond from a firm, and then resell the bond to either a firm or a consumer.

- Make sure your firm keeps enough cash to pay for all the bonds it has issued when the bonds mature. If the firm that sold the bond does not have enough cash to pay the face value of the bond when the bond matures, the program enters bond default mode and your firm will be turned over to a liquidator. In order to pay the bond, the liquidator will confiscate (first) enough inventory and (then if necessary) enough capital from the firm to pay the face value and a penalty. The bond default penalty is some percentage of the face value of the bond, chosen by your instructor, the default is 20 percent. For example, if the bond default penalty is 20% and you need to sell $450 of inventory to cover a bond, the liquidator will take from you inventory (or, if needed, inventory + capital) totaling 120% of $450, or $540.

- If the cash + inventory value + capital value are not sufficient enough to pay for the mature bond(s), your firm will go bankrupt, which means that you would be able to view your Firm Graphs, Firm Functions, and Firm Record pages, but that you would not be able to enter your Firm Actions page.

CONSUMERS

- Consumers receive utility from leisure and consuming two goods. The goal of the consumer is to maximize utility.

- Goods are consumed as soon as they are purchased. Consumers cannot resell goods after they have purchased them. Time not spent working for a firm is automatically consumed as leisure.

- Consumers start the game with some amount of cash specified by the instructor.

- Consumers might also be given some amount of income each period if the instructor has chosen that option.

- At the beginning of each period, each consumer is allocated some number of hours that can be consumed as leisure or spent working for firms.

- Consumers can earn income by giving up some of their leisure time to work for firms.

- Keep in mind that your firm will not see your consumer's offers to sell labor.

- Your consumer "owns" your firm. Your firm can transfer cash from itself to your consumer.

- At the beginning of each period the number of units consumed is reset to zero. Each participant is given a new allotment of leisure time. Only cash can be carried over from one period to the next.

- The utility for each period is calculated at the end of the period. All Periods utility is equal to the sum of the utilities from the completed periods, plus the Current Utility of the current period.

FIRMS

Producing Output and Maximizing Profit

- Firms start the game with some amount of cash and some number of units of capital specified by the instructor. Firms might receive smaller additional amounts of cash at the start of each period if the instructor has chosen that option.

- Firms can earn profits by producing output and selling it to consumers. The firm must buy labor from consumers in order to produce output. Keep in mind that if your consumer consumes the same good that your firm produces, you will not see the offers of goods to sell from your firm. In addition, your firm cannot see labor offers from its consumer.

- The amount of output produced is a function of current capital stock and the quantity of labor hired. Once labor is purchased, it is automatically used to produce output. The firm's labor time is reset to zero at the start of each period.

- Any unsold output in the firm's inventory is carried over into the next period, minus any depreciation in the inventory. Depreciation in the inventory is due to the output spoiling or becoming obsolete.

- The profits that are reported are accounting profits, not economic profits.

- Firms are able to distribute their profits to their consumer, in the form of dividends.

- In addition, firm's net worth is calculated. This is calculated as cash + value of inventory + value of capital stock + present discounted value of bonds. Until the good your firm produces is bought in the marketplace, the value of your firm's inventory is $0.

Purchasing Capital

- Your instructor has the option of allowing firms to purchase additional capital.
- When it is possible to buy more capital, the game uses a capital firm that buys labor from the consumers, produces capital, and then offers the capital for sale to the firms.
- The amount of capital your firm can purchase at any one time is limited to the total capital in stock. If your firm wants to purchase more capital than what is available, you must buy what is available and then wait for the capital firm to produce more capital.

- When a firm buys capital, the capital will not have an effect on the firm's output until the next period. Thus, you cannot buy capital in the last period.

- Depreciation is the amount of capital lost each year through the wear and tear of using the capital. In MarketSim, capital will not depreciate until the first period where capital purchases are allowed. After that, capital depreciation will occur at the end of every period. The firm's capital, minus depreciation, is carried over into the next period.

- In periods where you are not able to buy capital, the value of capital in your firm's net worth is $0. If you are allowed to purchase capital in the first period, then the value of capital will be $0 until five labor transactions have taken place. In future periods, once capital can be purchased, capital will very likely already have a value since the necessary five labor transactions will likely have occurred.

Changing Industries

- Your instructor has the option of allowing firms to change industries. To decide whether to change industries, you should check the graph on your firm's Graphs page showing the profits by industry.

- If you choose to change industries, your firm will produce the new product in the next period. When the change to the new industry occurs, all remaining inventory from your original industry will be lost. Also, your capital stock will decrease by a penalty (set by your instructor).

Strategy Tips

BOTH CONSUMERS AND FIRMS

- When you are viewing a particular page, click on the Help link on the top navigation bar and you will receive help for the page that you are currently viewing.

- To refresh a page to see if your offers have been accepted, click on a Refresh List button (if one is available), or right click on a page and choose "refresh." The program will also notify you of any acceptances of your offers if you navigate to a different page, or when you log into your game and hit the Home Page.

CONSUMERS

- At the beginning of the game, you won't know what wage rates firms will accept. Begin by offering a small number of units of labor for sale. That way, if the wage rate increases dramatically, you will not lose out by selling all your labor early at a low wage.

- If the wage rate changes during the period, check to see if your utility maximizing amount of leisure to sell has changed. You may want to change the amount you work as the wage rate changes. This in turn will change the amount of goods you will want to purchase.

- Your All Periods utility will be highest if you tend to spread your consumption more evenly over all of the periods.

- Remember to use the rule for utility maximization to help you decide what purchases to make.

FIRMS

- Remember your goal as a firm is to maximize profits by setting marginal revenue (MR) equal to marginal cost (MC).

- If you are able to hire labor and produce output so that that the additional revenue you receive from selling that additional output will be greater than the additional cost of hiring the labor, then you should buy the labor and sell the output.

- Your production function will obey the law of diminishing marginal returns, so the output gained from hiring an hour of labor will always be less than the output gained from hiring the previous hour.

- Remember that the price of output might change over the course of a period, so do not count on being able to charge a specific price for huge units of output.

- Given that consumer income is limited, it is unlikely you will be able to sell all of your firm's output in one offer to a single consumer. Consider making multiple offers of smaller amounts. Think about the units your consumer might like to buy and how much cash your consumer has on hand. It's best to make some offers of the good for small units.

- When making decisions about purchasing capital, experiment with different quantities of capital before deciding how much capital to buy.

- Recall that once every firm buys more capital, they will be able to produce more output with the same level of labor. What do you think might happen to the prices of goods as this occurs?

- Since your grade is more heavily weighted on consumer performance, it is helpful to raise your consumer's utility by transferring some dividends from your firm to your consumer.

Program Structure: An Overview of the Features

HOME PAGE AND BASIC STRUCTURE

When you log onto Adam's market, you will be taken to the Home Page (see Figure 28). On this page, you can view any messages from your instructor, the schedule of periods in the simulation, and the most recent 6 offers that have been accepted in the marketplace. On the bottom of the Home Page, in the "ticker panel," you can view the amount of both goods consumed by your consumer, the output produced by your firm, the industry your firm will participate in next period (if you have changed industries in the current period), the depreciation rate of capital (which appears only in periods where capital depreciation occurs, and that is only in periods where capital purchases are allowed), and the depreciation rate of inventory.

Figure 28: The Home Page

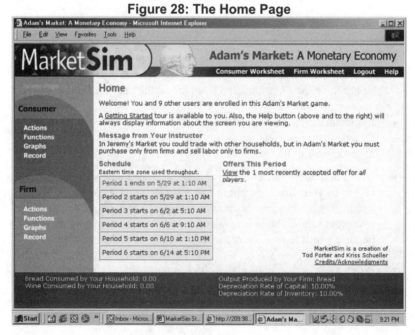

Note that colors referenced in this manual refer to the colors you will actually see on your screen while in the simulation. Screen captures in this manual print in black and white. The black bar across the top (underneath the title) is referred to as the **top navigation bar**. The links on the top navigation bar will open a separate window. Clicking on the links in this section will allow you to navigate to the Consumer Worksheet, Firm Worksheet, Logout or Help.

The blue panel on the left side of the screen is referred to as the **left navigation panel**. The links on the left navigation panel will take you to different pages within the game. The left navigation panel is accessible from any page in the game. The left navigation panel includes links for the consumer portion of the game—Actions, Bonds (if your professor has turned on the bond option), Functions, Graphs, and Record—and also includes links for the firm portion of the game—Actions, Bonds (if your professor has turned on the bond option), Functions, Graphs, and Record.

The dark blue bar across the bottom of the page is referred to as the **ticker panel** (or just the "ticker"). The information in the ticker varies with the page you are currently viewing.

ACCESSED FROM THE TOP NAVIGATION BAR

Consumer Worksheet

You will use this worksheet to plan your strategy as a consumer. This page will help you decide how many hours to work and how much of the two goods to purchase. Importantly, it is a *planning* tool and none of what you do here will be recorded as real actions. Remember that all of the calculations are based on the expected prices and wages. You are able to view the prices of the last five purchases for labor and the two goods.

Firm Worksheet

You will use this worksheet to plan your strategy as a firm. This page has only one worksheet (the Labor Worksheet), unless your instructor has allowed the purchase of capital (at which point the Capital Worksheet will also appear as an option). On the Labor Worksheet, you will decide how much labor to hire in order to maximize profits. On the capital worksheet, you will learn whether you should purchase more capital for use in the next period. As with the Consumer Worksheet, none of the actions on the Labor Worksheet or Capital Worksheet will be recorded as real actions. Remember that all of the calculations are influenced by the prices you specify.

Logout

Clicking on this link will log you out of the program; to get back in you will need to revisit the Student Log In page and successfully resubmit your User Name and Password.

Help

By clicking on the Help link, you will see information to help you with the specific page you are currently viewing. By clicking on Help from the home page, you can get information about the general program including some of the same tips and strategies outlined above in this Manual.

ACCESSED FROM THE LEFT NAVIGATION PANEL

Consumer Actions

This is where you can implement the strategy you planned on the Consumer Worksheet. There are a maximum of four actions to this page.

- At any time, you are able to offer your labor for sale or cancel any previous offers and to buy goods.
- Also, if your instructor has enabled the bonds market, your consumer can choose to buy bonds (lend money) and resell bonds. All actions taken on these pages are recorded.

Consumer Functions

This page displays your consumer's utility function and the utility functions of the other consumers.

Consumer Graphs

This link will navigate you to a graphs page with a dropdown menu. From the dropdown menu you can pick from a variety of graphs summarizing different results of your consumer and results of all consumers in the game. The information displayed includes information on output prices paid, wages, and utility.

Consumer Record

This page displays a summary of all the actions you have taken as a consumer.

Firm Actions

This is the page where you activate the strategy you planned on the worksheet pages. (Note that all actions taken on this page are recorded.) There are a maximum of eight actions to this page. At any time, you can:

- Purchase labor from the consumers
- Offer goods to sell output and cancel previous offers to sell output
- Distribute profits back to your consumer in the form of dividends

In addition, five other actions will appear if your instructor has enabled them.

- If your instructor enables the bond market, three more actions will appear:
  - o Your firm may post offers to sell a bond (borrow money),
  - o resell a bond your firm currently holds,
  - o and purchase bonds (lend money).
- If your instructor enables Industry Change, that action will appear.
- If your instructor enables Capital Purchase, that action will appear.

Firm Functions
This page displays your firm's production function and the production functions of firms in other industries.

Firm Graphs
This link will navigate you to a graphs page with a dropdown menu. From the dropdown menu you can pick from a variety of graphs summarizing different results of your firm and of all firms in the market. The information displayed includes information on production, units sold, inventory, output prices paid, wages and capital prices paid, profit, and firm net worth.

Firm Record
This page displays a summary of all the actions you have taken as a firm.

A DETAILED LOOK AT AN ADAM'S MARKET GAME

Consumer

THE TICKER PANEL

See Figure 29, which shows the ticker that displays on all Consumer pages (Consumer Worksheet, Actions, Functions, Graphs and Record). You will see information about the money you have at your disposal and your consumption in the current period.

- Under "Utility," you will see both your current utility and your All Periods utility, which is defined as current utility added to past utility from previous periods.
- Under "Current Consumption," you will see the amount of each good you have currently consumed, as well as the amount of leisure you are currently consuming.
- Under "Financial Assets," you can see how much cash your consumer has available. You can carry over cash from one period to another.

Figure 29: The Consumer Ticker

Utility	Current Consumption	Financial Assets
Current Period: 0.00	Bread: 0.00	Cash: $500.00
All Periods: 0.00	Wine: 0.00	
	Leisure: 1,000.00	

CONSUMER WORKSHEET

This link can be found in the top navigation bar. On this page (see Figure 30), you will be able to determine your utility maximizing amount of the two goods to buy, and leisure to sell. A separate window will open for the Consumer Worksheet. Since the Consumer Worksheet is in a separate window, you can keep this window open to use later when you visit the Consumer Action Page to enact your worksheet-planned strategy.

Figure 30: The Consumer Worksheet

Adam's Market Consumer Worksheet - Microsoft Internet Explorer

Adam's Market Consumer Worksheet   Help

Prices

Prices	Prices in Last Five Purchases				
Bread:	N/A	N/A	N/A	N/A	N/A
Wine:	N/A	N/A	N/A	N/A	N/A
Wage:	3.00	2.00	N/A	N/A	N/A

Refresh List

Consumption Options

Savings: ○ Deposit of [ ]
○ Withdrawal of [ ]

Leisure/Work Split: [95% / 5% ▼]   (Leisure Hours 950, Work Hours 50)

Bread/Wine Split: [5% / 95% ▼]   (5% of Expenditures for Bread, 95% for Wine)

Expenditures and Utility

	Bread	Wine	Leisure		
Units Consumed				Wage Income:	
Expenditures				Expenditures:	
MU				Utility:	
MU/P					

Utility	Current Consumption	Financial Assets
Current Period: 0.00	Bread: 0.00	Cash: $566.00
All Periods: 0.00	Wine: 0.00	
	Leisure: 970.00	

Help
You can access the Help page for the Consumer Worksheet at any time by clicking on the Help link at the top right of the page.

Prices
To calculate your consumption options you must specify the wage rate you expect to earn and the prices at which you will buy your goods. The Prices table also displays the prices and wages paid for the last five purchases. You typically will choose the lowest price listed.

Consumption Options
You can use the Consumption Options to investigate the different possible combinations of leisure and consumption.

- In the dropdown menu for leisure/work split, set the division between leisure and work. Combined with the wage rate set in the table above, the program will calculate the expected income.
- Then, in the dropdown menu for the wine/bread split select the percentage of your income you want to spend on the two goods.
- If you want to spend more than you will make by working the selected hours in the dropdown menu, then click the button "Withdrawal of." In the box, put the amount that you want to spend down your savings. What is your savings? Savings is the total of your current consumer cash plus your current firm cash (since MarketSim allows you to transfer firm cash to your consumer in the form of dividends). You have an option to "spend" (in the theoretical worksheet sense) this savings if you wish, by making a withdrawal.
- You also have the option to add to your savings by not spending all of your worksheet Wage Income. In that case, click the button "deposit of" and enter the amount you want to add to your savings in the box.

As you change the amount you plan to work and the amount you plan to spend on the two goods, your level of utility will change.

Expenditures and Utility
There are two versions of this table. The author of your primary economics text may approach the problem of utility maximization using marginal utility theory or may approach the problem of utility maximization using indifference curve analysis. Your instructor has chosen the appropriate version of Adam's market for you depending on which method is used in your text book. Thus, you see a different "Expenditures and Utility" table depending on the method you are using.

Expenditures and Utility (MUx/Px = MUy/Py)
Figure 30 shows this version of the Expenditures and Utility information. As seen in Figure 30, there are two Expenditures and Utility tables when this utility maximization rule is used.

- As you try different combinations of consumption under "Consumption Options," the left table will display the number of units purchased of each good and the expenditures for each good (including leisure). The table also shows the marginal utility (MU) and the marginal utility per dollar (MU/P) for each of your two goods consumed and leisure. You'll want to try different combinations of goods and leisure until you get roughly the same marginal utility per dollar from both goods and from leisure time. You always want to consume more of the item that has the highest marginal utility per dollar (you want to get the most value per dollar spent). Recall that utility is maximized where the marginal utilities per dollar are equal. Thus, when you have found the place where the marginal utilities per dollar are equal for the two goods and leisure, the utility should be at its highest value. Because the Leisure/Work split and Bread/Wine split is broken up into 5% increments, you might not get the MU/P exactly equal, but try to come as close as you possibly can.

- In the table to the right, you can see your wage income, your expenditures (which should equal your wage income unless you've deposited into savings or withdrawn cash from savings), and your level of utility if you were to consume that combination of goods specified in the consumption options at the prices listed in the Prices table.

Remember, since the Consumer Worksheet is in a separate window, you can keep this window open in order to recall the utility maximizing values.

After you have entered prices for the two goods and labor, you will see a link that says "show the Budget Line and Indifference Curve graph." When you choose to "Show," you will see the graphical representation of the information in the Expenditures and Utility tables. This graph shows a point on the budget line that represents the combination of goods being consumed. Some books use a curve to represent a particular level of utility and the tradeoff from trading one good for another (this curve is called an indifference curve). The goal is to maximize utility (to be on the highest curve possible), given the budget line. When the budget line is tangent to the curve, the consumer is maximizing utility. The curve will be tangent to the budget line when the MU/P is equal for the two goods. Although you have not learned about indifference curves, you can tell if you are maximizing your consumer's utility by looking for the tangencies in the graph.

Expenditures and Utility (MRS = Px/Py)

Figure 31 shows this version of the Expenditures and Utility information. There are three Expenditures and Utility tables when this utility maximization rule is used.

- As you try different combinations of consumption under "Consumption Options" for the leisure/work split and the bread/wine split, the left table in this section will display the number of units purchased of each good and the expenditures for each good (including leisure).

- In the right table, you can see your wage income, your expenditures (which should equal your wage income unless you've deposited into savings or withdrawn cash from savings), and your level of utility.

- Finally, the table on the bottom will show you the consumer's marginal rate of substitution (MRS) and relative price, given the different combinations. You'll want to try different combinations of goods and leisure until you find a point where the MRS is equal to the price ratio for all three situations (bread and wine, wine and leisure, and bread and leisure). When you find the place where MRS = Px/Py, then utility should be at its highest value.

Figure 31: The Consumer Worksheet Expenditure and Utility Information When the MRS = Px/Py Utility Maximization Rule Is Used in Your Game

Expenditures and Utility

Good	Units	Expenditures		
Bread			Wage Income:	
Wine			Expenditures:	
			Utility:	

Combination	MRS	Relative Price
Bread and Wine	0	
Leisure and Bread	0	
Leisure and Wine	0	

Since the consumer worksheet is in a separate window, you can keep this window open in order to recall the utility maximizing values.

After you have entered prices for the two goods and labor, you will see a link that says "show the Budget Line and Indifference Curve graph." When you choose to "Show," you will see the graphical representation of the information in the Expenditures and Utility tables. The graph shows a point on the budget line that represents the combination of goods being consumed. You can see the indifference curve, representing the level of utility at the consumption point. When the budget line is tangent to the indifference curve, the consumer is maximizing utility. You can view the budget line and indifference curve graph of the two goods, good X and leisure, and good Y and leisure. Ideally, you want to consume leisure and the other two goods such that you see tangencies in all three graphs.

CONSUMER ACTIONS

This link can be found in the left navigation panel. On the Action pages you will be able to carry out the actions that you figured out on the Consumer Worksheet page. Remember to keep the Consumer Worksheet window open in order to view your utility maximizing values of how many hours to work and how many units of each good to buy.

Offer Labor

When you first navigate to the Actions page, you will be in the "Offer Labor" section. (See Figure 32.) This page is where your consumer can offer labor to sell to firms.

Figure 32: Consumer Actions / Offer Labor

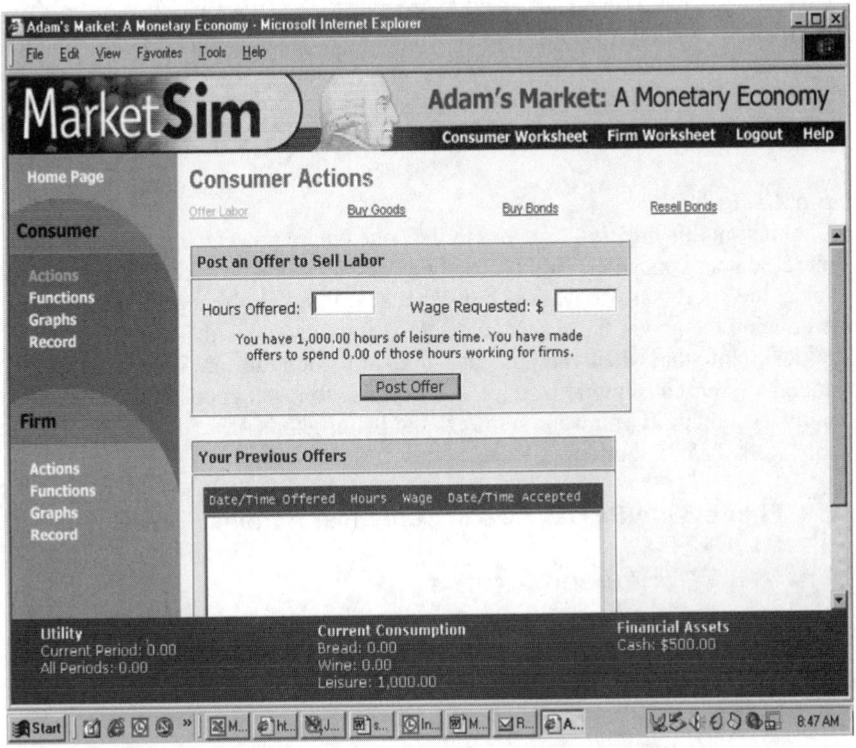

Post an Offer to Sell Labor

To post an offer to work for a firm, type in the number of hours you are willing to work and the wage you are asking in the appropriate text boxes in the table. To determine the wage to ask, you can navigate to the Graphs page and select the Wages graph from the dropdown menu. This will help you determine the going wage rates. In addition, you could navigate to the Firm Actions page and view the current wages requested from others. The graphical information tells you the wages of accepted offers. The Firm Actions page shows you the actual wage offers currently available.

Once you have entered your Hours Offered and Wage Rate, click the "Post Offer" button to make the offer available. Recall how many hours you determined you should work from the Worksheet window. It is probably best to offer your labor in smaller increments making sure that the total amount offered (and already bought) totals to the utility maximizing amount you should work. Remember that you need to retain a portion of your time for leisure time to maximize your utility. Offers that are not accepted before the end of the period are automatically cancelled.

Your Previous Offers

By default, this table lists all of the sell labor offers you have posted but others have not accepted. If you also want to see a history of your accepted offers, click on the "Show Accepted Offers" checkbox. To refresh the list, click on the "Refresh List" button (which is the way to see if any of the offers in the list have been accepted since you loaded this page). To cancel an offer, select the offer you wish to cancel and click on the "Cancel Offer" button.

Buy Goods

Clicking on this link will take you to the page where you can buy goods to help increase your consumer's utility. (See Figure 33.) Click on the radio buttons to select the good that you want to buy. The table lists the offers posted by firms producing the goods. To accept an offer, select it and click the "Buy Goods" button. Note that when you purchase units of a good they are immediately added to your consumption, so it is not possible to resell goods after you have purchased them. If you want to refresh the list of goods offered for sale, click on the "Refresh List" button.

Figure 33: A Partial View of Consumer Actions / Buy Goods

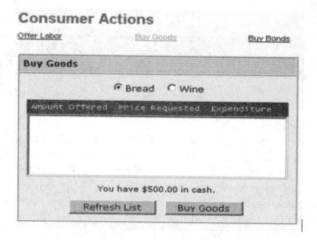

Buy Bonds

This link will only appear when your instructor has enabled the bonds market. Clicking on this link will take you to the page where your consumer is able to buy bonds. (See Figure 34.) The table in this section lists all of the bonds that are being offered for sale. To purchase a bond, select it and then click on "Buy Bond" button. The following characteristics of the bond are listed in the table.

- **Price** This is the amount you must pay for the bond. It is the amount you are lending to the seller of the bond.

- **Face Value** This is the amount that will be paid to whomever holds the bond when it matures.

- **Period Matures** At the end of the specified period the face value of the bond is deducted from the cash of the firm that originally issued the bond and is added to the cash of the firm or consumer that owns the bond.

- **Yield** This is a measure of the return received by the purchaser of the bond, expressed in percentage terms. The size of the yield depends on the difference between the purchase price and the face value, and the amount of time before the bond matures. For example, suppose a consumer bought a bond from a firm for $200 at the very end of period 3. If the bond matured at the end of period 4 and had a face value of $220, the bond would have a yield of 10%. The relevant calculation would be: $(220 - 200)/200 = 20/200 = 0.1 = 10\%$. The yield changes to reflect the fraction of the period left.

Figure 34: A Partial View of Consumer Actions / Buy Bonds

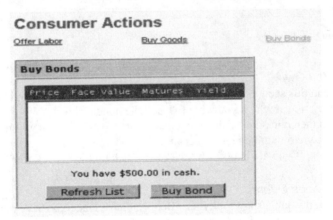

Resell Bonds

This link will only appear when your instructor has enabled the bonds market. Clicking on this link will take you to the page where you have the option of reselling bonds that you have purchased from a firm or a consumer. (See Figure 35.)

Figure 35: Consumer Actions / Resell Bonds

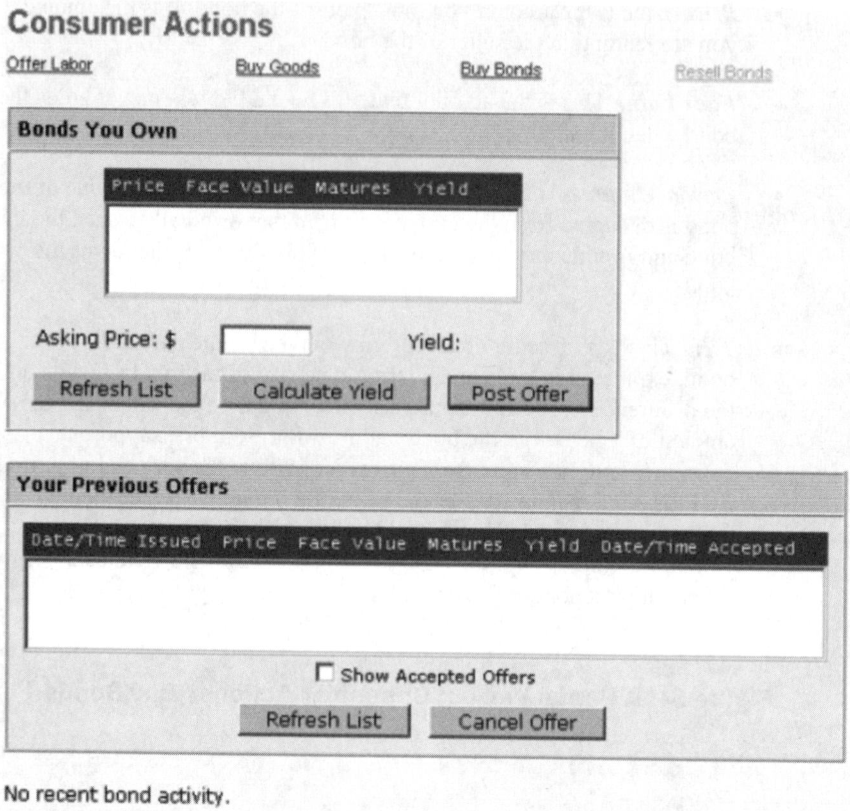

Consumer Actions

Offer Labor   Buy Goods   Buy Bonds   Resell Bonds

Bonds You Own

Price	Face Value	Matures	Yield

Asking Price: $ [   ]   Yield:

[Refresh List]   [Calculate Yield]   [Post Offer]

Your Previous Offers

Date/Time Issued	Price	Face Value	Matures	Yield	Date/Time Accepted

☐ Show Accepted Offers

[Refresh List]   [Cancel Offer]

No recent bond activity.

Bonds You Own

The table in this section lists all of the bonds you own. To sell a bond, select it, type in the price at which you want to resell the bond (in the "Asking Price" field), and then click the "Calculate Yield" button. The program will then display the yield that the new owner of the bond would receive, given your asking price. If you are happy with the offer, click on the "Post Offer" button.

Your Previous Offers

By default, this table shows all your offers you have made that have not been accepted by others. If you also want to see a history of your accepted offers, click on the "Show Accepted Offers" checkbox. To ensure your list is up-to-date, click the "Refresh List" button. You can cancel an offer to sell a bond if the offer has not yet been accepted. To do so, click on the offer you wish to cancel and click the "Cancel Offer" button.

CONSUMER FUNCTIONS

This link can be found in the left navigation panel. This page displays your consumer's utility function and the utility functions of the other consumers. (See Figure 36.) Note that you do not need to directly use these functions when participating in the game. You can use the Consumer Worksheet, which are based on the functions, to plan your strategy, and any actions you take automatically use these functions.

Figure 36: A Partial View of the Consumer Functions Page

Consumer Functions

Utility Function for Your Group (Group 1)

Utility Function
$U = 10.0 * (Bread^{0.5} * Wine^{0.2} * Leisure\ Time^{0.2})$

Utility Functions for Other Groups Involved in This Game

Group	Utility Function
2	$U = 10.0 * (Wine^{0.5} * Bread^{0.2} * Leisure\ Time^{0.2})$

CONSUMER GRAPHS

This link can be found in the left navigation panel. On this page, you will find a dropdown menu allowing you to choose which graph to display. (See Figure 37.) There are four possible graphs to display.

Figure 37: The Consumer Graphs Page, with the Dropdown Opened

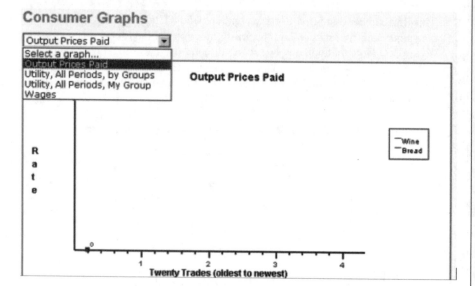

Output Prices Paid
The prices charged for the last twenty sales of each product.

Utility, All Periods, by Groups
This presents a bar chart displaying the "All Periods" utility (current utility added to past utility from previous periods) by group. The groups are sorted by both consumer utility group and the product you produce. The bar chart labels the maximum All Periods utility value and median All Periods utility value for each group. The median is the middle value in a set of numbers. For example, in the set of numbers: 10, 9, 8, 3, 3, the median value is 8.

Utility, All Periods, My Group
This presents a bar chart showing the rank of your All Periods utility compared to all other consumers in your group. The groups are sorted by both consumer utility group and the product you produce. This graph shows how your All Periods utility ranks compared to other similar consumers, who also happen to produce the same good as you do.

Wages
This presents a graph showing wage rates paid for the last twenty sales of labor. This graph is helpful in determining the wage rates to offer your labor for sale.

CONSUMER RECORD

This link can be found in the left navigation panel. This is the page where you can see a record of all your actions as a consumer since the start of the game. (See Figure 38.) If you have questions about why your level of utility has changed or about your consumer's cash balance, the first thing you should do is check your Consumer Record. At the top of the page, there is a dropdown menu for the periods. The page will always open to the record for the current period. If you wish to review your record from previous periods, simply choose a different period from the dropdown menu.

Figure 38: The Consumer Record at the Start of a Game

Consumer Record for Sasha Cat in Period: 1 ▾

Period Status
Open until 6/1 at 12:34 PM Eastern

Cash Balance
Starting Balance: $500.00 Current Balance: $500.00

Transaction	Date/Time	Units	Price	Amount	Cash Balance

Consumption

Transaction	Date/Time	Units	$ Amount
Bread Totals		0.00	$0.00
Wine Totals		0.00	$0.00
Initial Leisure		1000.00	
Current Leisure		1000.00	

Utility Calculation
Current Utility $= 10.0(\text{Bread}^{0.5})(\text{Wine}^{0.2})(\text{Time}^{0.2})$
(Group 1) $\quad = 10.0(0.0^{0.5})(0.0^{0.2})(1000.0^{0.2})$
$\quad = 0.0$

Bonds

Transaction	Date/Time	Period Issued	Matures	Price	Face Value

Cash Balance
This section displays the amount of cash you had at the start of the period, every change in your cash balance, and the current balance (or the balance at the end of the period). The "Amount" column in the table keeps track of the changes in cash as a result of the actions of your consumer. If your consumer has spent

cash through expenditures such as purchases of goods and bonds, then the values in the "Amount" column are shown in red. If your consumer has gained cash as a result of income from wages, dividends, or bond payments, then the values in the "Amount" column are shown in green. The last column, "Cash Balance," will increase with income additions and decrease with expenditures.

Consumption

This table shows the amounts consumed of the two goods and leisure time. Each individual purchase of a good is listed. The table also lists each block of time you worked for a firm, which records the reduction in the amount of time available for leisure.

Utility Calculation

This section shows your current level of utility given the consumption of leisure and your two goods.

Bonds

This table will be displayed only if your instructor has enabled the bond market for the period. The table lists bonds that you have bought. The bonds are assets, since they will provide you with income at some future time.

Firm

THE TICKER PANEL

See Figure 39, which shows the ticker that displays on all Firm pages (Firm Worksheet, Actions, Functions, Graphs and Record). You will see information about the production, cash, profit, and net worth of your firm.

- Under "Firm Measures," you will see your lifetime profit, your net worth, and what good your firm produces. Net Worth is defined as defined as cash + value of inventory + value of capital stock + present discounted value of bonds.
- Under "Inputs Used This Period," the ticker includes the amount of labor and capital your firm has used this period. The ticker also provides (see "New Capital Next Period") the amount if capital you have purchased in the current period—capital that will become available for use in the next period.
- Under "Financial Assets" you can see the cash of the firm and the net present value of any bonds the firm has issued.
- Under "Inventory," the firm's inventory of product is displayed.

Figure 39: The Firm Ticker

Firm Measures	Inputs Used This Period	Financial Assets
Lifetime Profit: $0.00	Labor: 0.00 Capital: 16.00	Cash: $500.00 Net PV, Bonds: $0.00
Net Worth: $500.00	New Capital Next Period	Inventory
Producing: Bread	0.00	0.00

FIRM WORKSHEET

A click on the Firm Worksheet link in the top navigation bar of the main window will open the Firm Worksheet, which can be seen in Figure 40. A separate window will open for the Firm Worksheet. Since the Firm Worksheet is in a separate window, you can keep this window open to use later when you visit the Firm Action Page to enact your worksheet-planned strategy.

Figure 40: The Firm Worksheet (Defaulted to the Labor Worksheet)

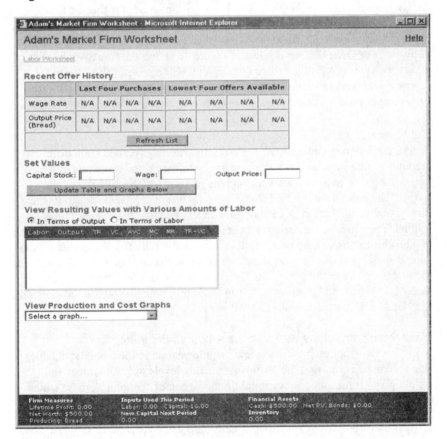

Help

You can access the Help page for the Firm Worksheet at any time by clicking on the Help link at the top right of the Firm Worksheet page.

Labor Worksheet

Figure 40 shows a "Labor Worksheet" link near the top of the page. (If Capital Purchases are currently allowed in a game, to the right of the "Labor Worksheet" link you will see a "Capital Worksheet" link. Even when this Capital Worksheet link appears, though, the Worksheet will always open to the Labor Worksheet.) The Labor Worksheet is where you can *figure out* how much labor the firm should hire in order to maximize profits (remember that no actions are actually *recorded* from your work on the Labor Worksheet).

Recent Offer History

To help you estimate the price at which you can sell your output and the wage at which you can purchase labor, this table shows the values for the last four accepted offers and the currently-available (i.e. posted but not yet accepted) four lowest offers. Figure 40 shows "N/A" for the "Last Four Purchases" and for the "Lowest Four Offers." This is because Figure 40 shows the screen at the start of a game, where no offers have been made. You will also see "N/A" for the "Lowest Four Offers" at the start of each new period, since at the end of the previous period any outstanding offers were canceled by MarketSim.

Set Values

Before the program can estimate the costs and revenues earned from different amounts of output you must specify your capital stock, the wage rate at which you will need to pay your workers, and the price at which you will sell the output. The default for "capital stock" is your current capital stock. In this text box, you have the option of changing the level of capital to see how output might change in a single period with new capital. Remember, however, that capital will last more than one period and to see the full effect of an increase in capital stock, you should look at the capital worksheet. Using the information on the prices and wage rates from the last set of accepted offers, type in your desired wage rate and price of output in the appropriate text boxes and click on the "Update Table and Graphs Below" button.

View Resulting Values with Various Amounts of Labor

You have two choices in how to view the information in the table. Both tables in this section help you find the profit-maximizing levels of employment and output given some amount of capital. In the jargon of economics, these tables help you find the short run profit-maximizing level of output. In the short run, firms have a fixed amount of capital to work with but can vary the amount of labor they employ. In the game, the length of the short run depends on whether you can purchase capital or not. If you cannot purchase capital, you are always dealing with a "short-run" situation. If you can purchase capital, the short run lasts until the end of the current period, because you cannot change the amount of capital in the current period, but you can purchase additional capital for use in the next period. Remember that in the short run firms add to their profits whenever revenues exceed variable costs.

- Clicking on the radio button "In Terms of Output" will show cost and revenues for different levels of output. In this table the most important values are marginal cost (MC) and marginal revenue (MR). Firms maximize profits in the short run by hiring up to the point where the additional cost from producing another unit of output (MC) equals the revenue from producing another unit of output (MR). Also keep in mind the shut-down rule, which states that a firm should not produce anything if MR is less than average variable cost (AVC) for all levels of output.
- Clicking on the radio button "In Terms of Labor" helps you find the profit-maximizing level of output in terms of employment. In this case you want to compare the wage rate and marginal revenue product (MRP). Marginal revenue product measures how much revenues rise when an additional unit of labor is hired; the wage measures how much costs rise when an additional unit of labor is hired. To maximize profits, firms should hire labor up to the point where MRP equals the wage. Note that the profit-maximizing levels of output and employment using MR and MC will match the levels found using the wage and MRP.

View Production and Cost Graphs
In this section, you can choose to view graphs based on the information in the previous tables. You can select to display four different types of graphs from the dropdown menu.

- The Marginal and Average Product graph will give you some idea of the type of production function you have. The firm should be producing the level of output where the distance between Variable Cost and Total Revenue are the largest. Viewing this graph might help to see if your firm is maximizing profit.
- The AVC, MC, and MR graph is the most helpful in terms of viewing the profit maximizing level of output. Your firm should produce where the MC and MR graphs cross. However, your firm should not produce if the MR graph is below the AVC graph at the level of output you choose to produce.
- Finally, the profit maximizing choice can be seen in the MRP and Wage graph where those two curves cross.

Capital Worksheet
If Capital Purchases are currently allowed in a game, to the right of the "Labor Worksheet" link you will see a "Capital Worksheet" link. Figure 41 shows this

Capital Worksheet link selected, with the Capital Worksheet page showing. From this page you will be able to determine how much capital to buy. This link on the worksheet only appears in periods when you are able to purchase capital and after five offers of labor have been accepted so that the capital producer is able to determine the price of capital.

Figure 41: The Capital Worksheet Page of the Firm Worksheet

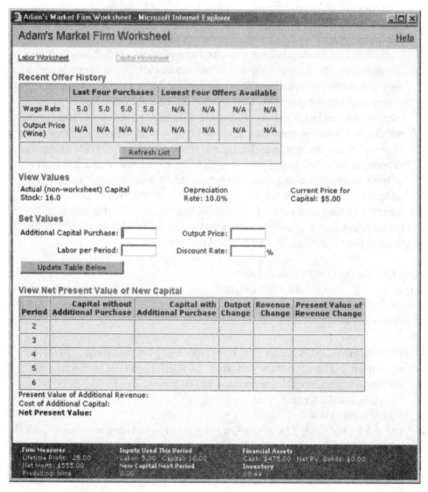

Recent Offer History

To help you estimate the price at which you can sell your output, this table shows the values for the last four accepted offers and the current four lowest offers. It is the same table from the Labor Worksheet. Again, if you see only N/A for data (such as you see in Figure 41 for the Lowest Four Offers Available and Output Price for Wine) just start somewhere and see what happens.

View Values
The information here tells you your current capital stock, the depreciation rate of capital, and the current price for capital.

Set Values
This section of the worksheet contains four text boxes.

- Enter the amount of capital you are considering buying in the "Capital Purchase" text box.
- Enter the labor you anticipate using per period in the "Labor per Period" text box. The amount of labor you anticipate using can be some combination of what you have currently been using to maximize profits and some possible increase to take account for the fact that you will most likely be using more labor as you have additional capital to use.
- In the text box labeled "Output Price," enter a value at which you would like to sell future output. Keep in mind that as firms purchase capital, every firm will become more productive and supply of the product will increase. Thus, the previous going rate for output might not reflect the going rate for output after capital purchases have been made. This is something of a guessing game. It is better to be conservative.
- Finally, enter a discount rate you would like to use in determining net present value. Your professor might tell you what value to use for this text box.

After you have entered values in all four boxes, click the "Update Table Below" button.

View Net Present Value of Capital
This table helps you decide if you can increase your profits by purchasing capital. Additional capital will increase output and revenue for the rest of the game, so you need to compare the cost of the capital against the total value of the additional revenue in all the remaining periods.

- The first column in the table displays the period.

- The second column in the table displays your capital stock for each period assuming you do not buy any capital. Economists refer to the rate at which capital wears out as the depreciation rate. If the depreciation rate has been set to zero, the amount of capital listed in this column will be the same for all the periods. If, on the other hand, the depreciation rate is, say, 5 percent, the stock of capital will decrease by 5 percent each period.

- The third column shows the amount of capital you would have if you did purchase the additional capital specified above the table in Set Values / "Additional Capital Purchase."

- The fourth column shows how much additional output would be produced if you purchased the additional capital, given the amount of labor you said you would hire.

- The fifth column shows the additional revenue you would receive, given the additional output and the output price you specified.

- The last column discounts the additional revenues. Economists typically assume that money received in the future is not as valuable as money received in the present. If you pick a discount rate of 5 percent, it means that you believe that 95 cents in the current period has the same value as a dollar received in the next period.

In deciding whether to purchase capital, you should compare the difference between the present value of the additional revenue from buying the capital and the cost of purchasing the capital. Economists would call the difference the net present value of the additional capital. If the net present value is positive, purchasing the capital will increase your profits if your estimate of the output price is correct.

If you decide you can add to your profits by purchasing more capital, you should go back to the Labor Worksheet page and see if the additional capital will change your profit-maximizing level of employment.

FIRM ACTIONS

This page is where you can implement the strategy you planned on the Firm Worksheet pages. There are a maximum of eight actions to this page.

- At any time, you are able to access Buy Labor, Offer Goods, and Distribute Dividends.
- If you are in a period where capital purchases are allowed and if MarketSim has been able to establish a price for capital (something that requires five labor transactions in the game), then you will be able to access Buy Capital.
- If you are in a period where industry change is allowed, you will be able to access Change Industry.
- If you are in a period where bond purchases are allowed, you will be able to access Issue Bonds, Buy Bonds, and Resell Bonds.

Buy Labor

When you first navigate to the Firm Actions page, you will be in the section "Buy Labor." (See Figure 42.) The table in this section displays the consumers' offers to sell labor time. To accept an offer, select the offer and click the "Accept Offer" button. The labor purchased is then automatically used to produce output (it is not possible to "store" labor hours). In order to see any new offers of labor, click the "Refresh List" button.

Figure 42: A Partial View of the Firm Actions / Buy Labor Page

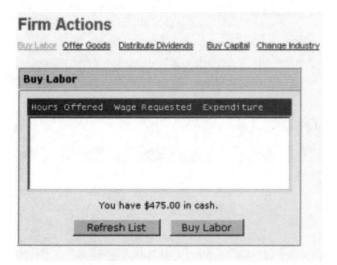

Offer Goods
Clicking on this link displays the page where you can sell your output to consumers. (See Figure 43.)

Figure 43: A Partial View of the Firm Actions / Offer Goods Page

Post an Offer to Sell Goods

Enter the number of units you want to sell and the price you are asking. When you have entered all of the information, click the "Post Offer" button. Any offer that is not accepted before the end of the period is automatically cancelled.

Your Previous Offers

In this table you will see all your firm's current offers to sell output. To cancel an offer, click on the offer you want to cancel and then click the "Cancel Offer" button. To refresh the list of offers, click the "Refresh List" button, which will also wake up the MarketSim alert system, letting you know if any of your past offers have been accepted. The "Show Accepted Offers" feature allows you to see your past offers that were previously accepted.

Distribute Dividends

Clicking on this link will take you to a page where you can transfer cash from your firm to your consumer. (See Figure 44.) Enter the amount of money you wish to transfer and click the "Distribute Dividends" button.

Figure 44: A Partial View of the Firm Actions / Distribute Dividends Page

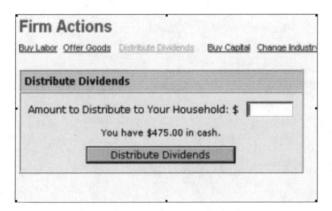

Buy Capital

This link will only appear in periods when you are able to buy capital. The capital producer must see five recorded purchases of labor before it is able to produce capital and determine the price of capital. So, this link will not appear in the initial period in which you are able to buy capital until after there have been five purchases of labor. The game assumes there is a producer of capital who hires labor from the consumers, makes capital, and then sells the capital to firms. Whenever a firm buys capital, the capital producer takes the money from the sale and tries to buy labor to produce new capital.

See Figure 45. The table displays the current price of capital and the number of units of capital available for purchase. Remember to go to the Capital Worksheet to determine how much capital your firm should buy this period. Then, enter the amount of capital you wish to buy in the "Units to Buy" field and click on the "Buy Capital" button. The number of units you buy will be added to your capital stock at the start of the next period.

If there is no capital available, it probably means that another participant has purchased all of the capital. Similarly, if you purchase all remaining available capital, there might be a time when no capital is available to purchase. If you wish to purchase more, wait until the capital producer has produced more capital.

Figure 45: A Partial View of the Firm Actions / Buy Capital Page

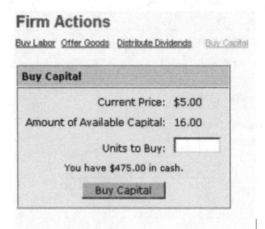

The price of capital is based on the cost of labor hired and the production function for capital. For example, if it takes two units of labor to produce a unit of capital and the wage rate is $10, capital will cost $20 per unit.

Change Industry

This link will only appear in periods when you are able to change industries. If firms in another industry are earning significantly higher profits than the firms in your industry, you might want to consider changing industries.

See Figure 46. To change industries, select the industry you wish to enter from the list. When you select an industry other than the one in which you are currently producing, you will receive information about the penalty for changing and a reminder to get rid of all your current inventory before the current period ends. If you are sure you want to change industries, click the "Change Industry" button. Two things will then happen.

- On the ticker for the Home Page, "Industry Next Period" information will appear.

- Starting in the next period, you will be producing the product you selected.

Figure 46: The Firm Actions / Change Industry Page

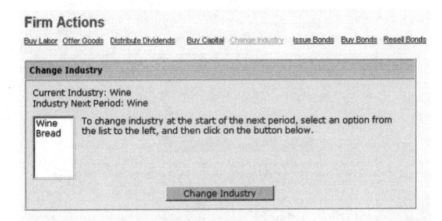

There are two consequences to changing industries.

- First, your inventory will be set to zero when you start producing the new product (i.e. when the next period begins) because you cannot carry over inventory from your old industry. In other words, if you are producing bread and in period 3 and indicate you want to change to producing wine, none of your bread inventory can be carried over into period 4. In this case you would want to have sold all of your bread inventory by the end of period 3.

- The second consequence to changing industries is there will be a reduction in your stock of capital. The reduction in capital is justified since changing industries would most likely cause a need for different equipment and retraining of workers. The percentage reduction is set by your instructor and is indicated when you choose the new industry from the list.

Issue Bonds
This link will only appear when the bond market is turned on. Issuing bonds is a way for your firm to borrow money. You might decide to borrow money so you can invest in additional capital. If you borrow to purchase capital, you want to be sure that the return on your investment is greater than the amount you have to pay to borrow the money. See Figure 47.

Figure 47: The Firm Actions / Issue Bonds Page

Firm Actions

Buy Labor Offer Goods Distribute Dividends   Buy Capital Change Industry   Issue Bonds   Buy Bonds Resell Bonds

Issue a New Bond

Asking Price: $ [   ]   Matures at End of Period: [1 ▾]

Face Value: $ [   ]   Yield:

[Calculate Yield]   [Post Offer]

Note: If you do not have enough cash to pay for the bond at its maturity,
the necessary quantity of (first) Inventory and (then) Capital will be liquidated.
Liquidation carries a 15% charge on top of the necessary funds to pay for the bond.

Your Previous Offers

Date/Time Issued	Price	Face Value	Matures	Yield	Date/Time Accepted
-Accepted Offers-					

☑ Show Accepted Offers

[Refresh List]   [Cancel Offer]

No recent bond activity.

Issue A New Bond

Before issuing a new bond, you want to first find the yield on the bond you are
going to offer. Enter the amount you want to borrow in the "Asking Price" field.
Then, enter the amount you will pay to whomever holds the bond when it
matures in the "Face Value" field. Finally, determine the period in which the
bond will mature. Then, click on the "Calculate Yield" button. The yield is a
measure of the return received by the purchaser of the bond, expressed in
percentage terms. The size of the yield depends on the difference between the
purchase price and the face value, and the amount of time before the bond
matures. If you are happy with the yield amount of the bond, then you might
click on the "Post Offer" button to post the bond. Be careful to make sure you
will have enough cash to pay for the bond at its maturity. If you don't have
enough cash to pay the holder of the bond when it matures, the game's
"collection agency" will sell off part or all of your firm's inventory (first) and
capital (second, if necessary) until it has raised enough money to cover the face
value of the bond. The default penalty for liquidation is 20% of the bond's face
value (or a different percentage set by your instructor). If the total value of your
firm is less than the value of the bond and the penalty, your firm will be

declared bankrupt and will be shut down for the remainder of the game, which means you will be able to access Firm Worksheet, Firm Functions, Firm Graphs, and Firm Record, but that you will not be able to access Firm Actions.

Your Previous Offers

This table shows all your offers you have made. To ensure your list is up-to-date, click the "Refresh List" button. You can cancel an offer to issue a bond if the offer has not yet been accepted. To do so, click on the offer you wish to cancel and then click the "Cancel Offer" button.

Buy Bonds

This link will only appear if the bond market is turned on. Purchasing bonds is a way for your firm to lend money. See Figure 48. The table in this section lists all of the bonds that are being offered for sale. To purchase a bond, click on the bond you wish to buy and then click the "Accept Offer" button.

Figure 48: A Partial View of the Firm Actions / Buy Bonds Page

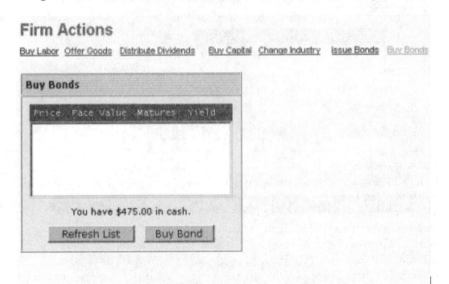

The following characteristics of the bond are listed in the table:

- **Price** This is the amount you must pay for the bond. It is the amount you are lending to the seller of the bond.

- **Face Value** This is the amount that will be paid to whomever holds the bond when it matures.

- **Period Matures** At the end of the maturing period, the face value of the bond is deducted from the cash of the firm that originally issued the bond, and is added to the cash of the firm or consumer that owns the bond.

- *Yield* A measure of the return received by the purchaser of the bond, expressed in percentage terms. The size of the yield depends on the difference between the purchase price and the face value, and the amount of time before the bond matures.

Resell Bonds

This link will only appear if the bond market is turned on. It allows you the option of reselling bonds that you have purchased. See Figure 49.

Figure 49: The Firm Actions / Resell Bonds Page

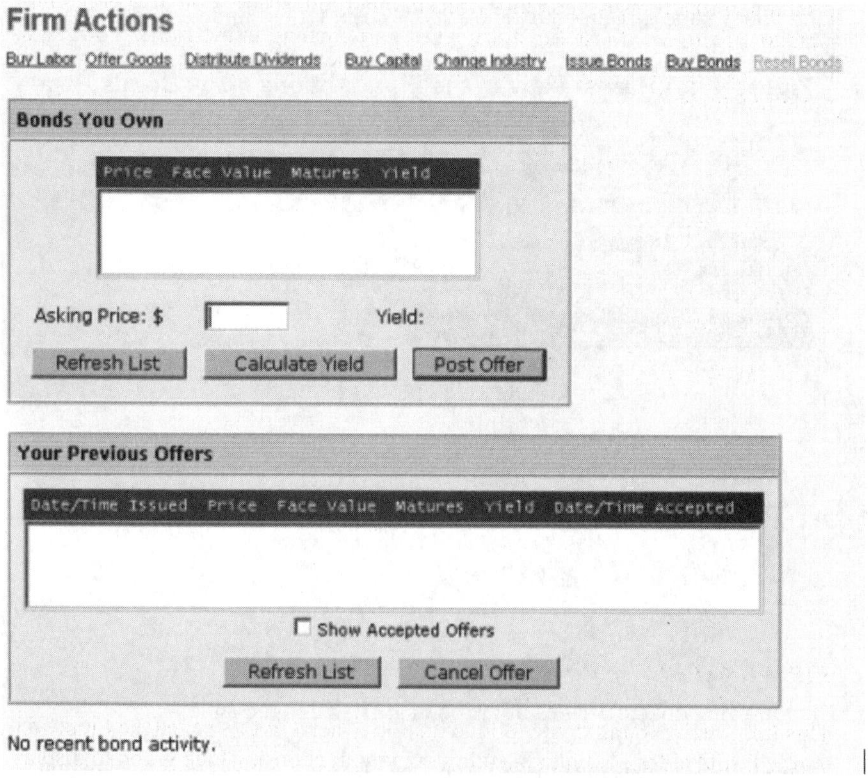

Bonds You Own

This table lists all of the bonds you own. To sell a bond, select the bond you wish to sell, and enter the "Asking Price" at which you want to sell the bond. Before you click the "Post Offer" button, you might want to click the "Calculate

Yield" button to see the yield to the new owner of the bond, given your asking price. Once you have decided to resell the bond, click the "Post Offer" button.

Your Previous Offers

This table shows all your offers you have made. To ensure your list is up-to-date, click the "Refresh List" button. You can cancel an offer to resell a bond if the offer has not yet been accepted. To do so, click on the offer you wish to cancel and click the "Cancel Offer" button.

FIRM FUNCTIONS

This link can be found in the left navigation panel. This section displays your firm's production function for output. (See Figure 50.) It also displays the production functions of the other firms in other industries. Note that you do not need to directly use these functions when participating in the game. You can use the Firm Worksheet to plan your strategy, and the Firm Worksheet is based on these functions.

Figure 50: The Firm Functions Page

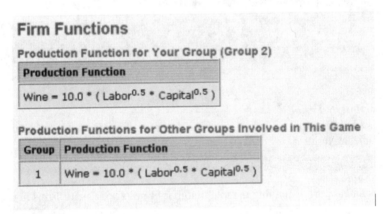

Firm Functions

Production Function for Your Group (Group 2)

Production Function
Wine = $10.0 * (Labor^{0.5} * Capital^{0.5})$

Production Functions for Other Groups Involved in This Game

Group	Production Function
1	Wine = $10.0 * (Labor^{0.5} * Capital^{0.5})$

FIRM GRAPHS

This link can be found in the left navigation panel. On this page (see Figure 51), you will find a dropdown menu allowing you to choose which graph to display. There are seven possible graphs to display.

Figure 51: Firm Graphs

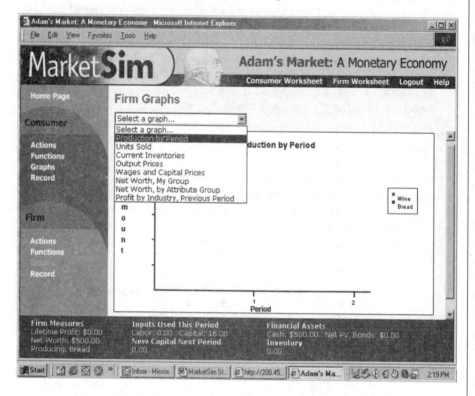

Production by Period
This is a bar chart displaying the total number of units produced by all of the firms in each industry for each period.

Units Sold
This is a bar chart displaying the total number of units sold by all firms in each industry for each period.

Current Inventories
This is a bar chart displaying current inventories for each industry.

Output Prices
This graph displays the prices charged for the last twenty sales of each product.

Wages and Capital Prices
This graph displays wage rates paid for the last twenty sales of labor and prices paid for the last twenty sales of capital.

Net Worth, My Group
This is a bar chart displaying the rank of your firm's net worth (defined as cash + value of inventory + value of capital stock + present discounted value of bonds) compared to all other firms in your industry group.

Net Worth, by Attribute Group
Each of the two-tone bars in the graph represents a different industry. The height of the bar equals the net worth of the firm with the highest net worth in that industry. The height of the dividing line between the two colors is equal to the net worth of the firm with the median net worth in that industry.

Profit by Industry, Previous Period
This is a bar chart displaying the profit (previous period) by industry. The maximum profit value and median profit value for each industry group are labeled in the chart.

Figure 52: The Firm Record

Firm Record for Emanuel Mansen in Period: 1 ▾

Period Status
Open until 6/1 at 12:34 PM Eastern

Cash Balance
Starting Balance: $500.00 Current Balance: $475.00

Transaction	Date/Time	Units	Price	Amount	Cash Balance
Bought Labor	5/28 at 9:57 AM	1.00	$5.00	$5.00	$495.00
Bought Labor	5/28 at 9:57 AM	1.00	$5.00	$5.00	$490.00
Bought Labor	5/28 at 9:57 AM	1.00	$5.00	$5.00	$485.00
Bought Labor	5/28 at 9:57 AM	1.00	$5.00	$5.00	$480.00
Bought Labor	5/28 at 9:57 AM	1.00	$5.00	$5.00	$475.00

Capital Stock
Current Capital Stock: 16.00

Description	Date/Time	Units	Capital Stock

Inventory
Starting Inventory: 0.00 Current Inventory: 89.44

Transaction	Date/Time	Labor Used	Amount	Inventory
Produced Wine	5/28 at 9:57 AM	1.00	40.00	40.00
Produced Wine	5/28 at 9:57 AM	1.00	16.57	56.57
Produced Wine	5/28 at 9:57 AM	1.00	12.71	69.28
Produced Wine	5/28 at 9:57 AM	1.00	10.72	80.00
Produced Wine	5/28 at 9:57 AM	1.00	9.44	89.44

Output Calculation

Current Wine Production
(Group 2)
$$= 10.0(L^{0.5})(K^{0.5})$$
$$= 10.0(5.0^{0.5})(16.0^{0.5})$$
$$= 89.44$$

Bonds

Transaction	Date/Time	Period Issued	Matures	Price	Face Value

Cash Balance

This table displays the changes in the amount of cash held by the firm. Expenditures, such as purchases of labor, purchases of capital, purchases of bonds, and distribution of dividends are shown in red in the column labeled "amount." Revenue, either from the sale of output or bond payments, is shown in green in the column labeled "Amount."

Inventory

Changes in the amount of output held in inventory are recorded in this section. Additions to the inventory from the production of additional output are shown in green in the column labeled "Amount." Reductions in inventory from the sale of output are shown in red in the column labeled "Amount."

Capital Stock

This table displays the changes in the firm's stock of capital. The table lists any loss of capital due to depreciation, and also lists additions to the capital stock from purchases in the previous period.

Inventory

This table shows any changes in inventory. Additions to inventory from production of the good are shown in green in the "Amount" column. Deletions to inventory due to the sale of the good are shown in red in the "Amount" column.

Output Calculation

This section shows your firm's level of output given the current amount of labor hired and capital used.

Bonds

This table will be displayed in periods where the bond market is enabled. It lists bonds you have bought (which will provide you with income at some future time) and bonds you have issued (which you will have to pay off at some future time). Bonds you hold are assets and bonds you have issued are liabilities. The color green in the table reflects assets and the color red reflects the liabilities. For example, if your firm issues a bond, then the price will be in green since this is money that you currently have as a result of issuing the bond, whereas the numbers in the column "Face Value" will be in red to reflect the fact that you will have to pay that amount when the bond matures.

LEARNING ACTIVITIES & EXERCISES

The purpose of these exercises is to illustrate the principles you are learning in class using Adam's Market: A Monetary Economy. For these activities, we have assumed the goods produced and consumed are bread and wine. If your professor has chosen a different group of goods, simply mentally replace those goods for these words. The exercises are organized into nine topic areas:

1. Circular Flow
2. Utility Maximization with Money
3. Labor Supply
4. Profit-maximizing Level of Output in the Short Run
5. Profit-Maximizing Level of Employment in the Short-Run
6. Depreciation
7. Profit-maximizing Level of Capital
8. Entry and Exit
9. Bonds

Each topic begins with a brief discussion of the relevant concepts and their theoretical basis, and is followed by a set of activities that demonstrate how to use the concepts while participating in the game. The goal is to show you how to apply economic theory to solve real world problems.

1. Circular Flow

Virtually every economics textbook has a diagram that shows the circular relationship between goods, resources, and payments between consumers and firms. Sometimes this diagram does not occur until the macroeconomics section of the textbook. Locate the circular diagram in your textbook.

Adam's Market is a perfect example of the circular flow diagram. As consumers, we sell our labor (a resource) to firms. Firms then use the labor (and capital) to produce output (a good). Firms then sell these goods to consumers. This process completes the circular flow of goods and resources. Similarly, there is also a flow of money. Consumers spend their incomes on goods, which gives the firms revenue. Firms use the revenue to buy resources (or factors) and thus make payments to the consumers. Payments by firms to the labor market give consumer income. Consumers then use the income to purchase goods, and so on.

Activity 1: Identifying Output and Inputs
Click on the Firm Functions link from the left navigation panel. Identify your firm's production function. What is your firm's output? What are your firm's factors?

Activity 2: Flow of Goods and Resources

Click on the link to the Consumer Action page from the left navigation panel. On this page you have an opportunity to sell your labor to firms and to purchase goods from firms. Describe, using the specific goods in your game, the circular flow of goods and resources. Begin your explanation with your consumer.

Activity 3: Flow of Money

Click on the link to the Firm Action page from the left navigation panel. On this page, you have the opportunity to buy labor to produce goods and then offer your product to sell to consumers. Describe, using the specific goods in your game, the circular flow of money. Begin your explanation with the firm.

Activity 4: Dividend Payments to Consumers

Click on the link to the Firm Action page from the left navigation panel. On this page, you have the opportunity to distribute dividends to your consumer. What do you think would happen to the circular flow of money if the option to distribute dividends did not exist? Explain in what way the distribution of dividends follows the circular flow model.

2. Utility Maximization with Money

In your text, you have encountered the problem of consumer equilibrium or utility maximization. There are different ways to approach this problem. The author of your text might approach the problem in terms of marginal utility or in terms of marginal rate of substitution. On the consumer worksheet page, scroll down to the table "Consumption Options". Next to that title, you will see either "Expenditure, Utility Calculations ($MUx/Px = MUy/Py$)" or "Expenditure, Utility Calculations ($MRS = Px/Py$)". Both approaches allow for utility maximization. If you are using the $MUx/Px = MUy/Py$ method, please do the problems in section 2.1 of this chapter. If you are using the $MRS = Px/Py$ Method, please skip to section 2.2 of this chapter. With either approach, the end result is the same, so there is no need to worry about not learning the other approach.

2.1. UTILITY MAXIMIZATION ($MUX/PX = MUY/PY$)

In class, you have learned about the utility of a consumer. **Utility** is defined as the total satisfaction an individual receives from consuming a particular amount of goods (sometimes called a bundle of goods). **Marginal Utility (MU)** is the additional satisfaction (or additional utility) a consumer gets from consuming an additional unit of the good. Usually consumers experience diminishing marginal utility, where each successive unit of the good gives smaller and smaller incremental increases to utility. The law of diminishing marginal utility then says that with each additional unit of a good consumed, the marginal utility of that good decreases. For example, consider Table 13.

Table 13

Quantity of good X	Utility	**Marginal Utility of good X**
0	0	—
1	28	**28**
2	50	**22**
3	70	**20**

If the first two columns were given, we could calculate the third column as the change in utility divided by the change in the quantity of good X. Notice that Marginal Utility falls immediately. Some students think the law of diminishing marginal utility says utility will fall. Notice that utility is increasing, but at smaller and smaller increments. The law of diminishing marginal utility is apparent in your every day life. Do you think you obtain as much satisfaction from eating your fourth or fifth piece of bread as you did from eating your first?

A consumer's goal is to maximize utility. In order to maximize utility in the game, a consumer must spend all of his or her income. A consumer's **budget line** shows all the possible combinations of two goods the consumer can afford to buy, with given prices and income. For example, if a consumer spends all of his or her income on two goods, X and Y, and the price of good X is $5, the price of good Y is $2, and the consumer has $50 to spend, then Table 14 reflects some of the points on the consumer's budget line.

Table 14

Quantity of good X	Quantity of good Y
10	0
8	5
6	10
4	15
2	20
0	25

Graphing these points, with quantity of good X on the X axis and quantity of good Y on the Y axis, will yield a downward sloping graph with a slope of -2.5. The slope of the budget line reflects the ratio of the prices.

In order to discuss utility maximization (called consumer equilibrium in some texts), we must introduce the concept of **marginal utilities per dollar (MU/P),** which is defined as the marginal utility divided by the price of the good. A consumer maximizes his or her utility by setting the marginal utilities per dollar of goods equal while spending all of his or her income. If we have three goods, X, Y, and Z, then the consumer would maximize utility when all the income has been spent and the $MU_x/P_x = MU_y/P_y = MU_z/P_z$, where P is the price of good X, Y, or Z. In the game, the consumer chooses between three goods: leisure, and two other goods that are produced by firms. Although the actual name of the good can change, we will use bread and wine throughout the game. If you are consuming different goods than bread and wine, simply replace the words bread and wine with the names of your goods.

Activity 1: Points on a budget line
Click on the link to the Consumer Worksheet on the top navigation bar. Set the wage rate equal to 10, the price of bread equal to 8 and the price of wine equal to 5. Let's assume you begin with 100 hours of leisure. Under Consumption Options, choose to split leisure and work by choosing to spend 60 % of your time on leisure and 40 % of your time working. Begin with 5% spent on bread and 95% spent on wine. Increase the percentage spent on bread until you have reached the highest utility for the given choice of leisure and work; the marginal utilities per dollar for bread and wine should be close to equal (since you are holding the number of hours of leisure constant, the MU/P for leisure might not equal the MU/P for bread and wine). Show that the amount of bread and amount of wine that you should buy are on the budget line.

Activity 2: Shifts in Budget Lines
Click on the link to the Consumer Worksheet page on the top navigation bar. Set the wage rate equal to 10, the price of bread equal to 8 and the price of wine equal to 5. In the leisure/work split under Consumption Options, begin by choosing to spend 60% of your time on leisure and 40% of your time working. (Assuming you have 100 hours to allocate, you will use 60 hours for leisure and work 40 hours.) In the bread/wine split, begin with 5% of your expenditures spent on bread and 95% spent on wine.

    A. What is your income? Graph the consumer's budget line for the two goods (bread and wine), given income and prices. (You may check your answer – in terms of the endpoints- by clicking on "Show" link from "Show the Budget Line and Indifference Curve graph" option at the bottom of the Consumer Worksheet Page. Recall that this link will not appear unless you have entered prices in the text boxes at the top of the Consumer Worksheet. Choose the graph for bread and wine to verify your answer.)

    B. Now change the amount of leisure to 40 (and the amount of work to 60 hours). On your same graph as in part A, graph the consumer's new budget line. What has happened to the budget line? Explain. (You may check your answer as above in part A.)

Activity 3: MUx/Px = MUy/Py

Click on the link to the Consumer Worksheet page from the top navigation bar. Set the prices of the two goods and the wage rate equal to $5. In the leisure/work split under Consumption Options, begin by choosing to spend 80 hours of leisure and 20 hours of work. In the bread/wine split, begin with 5% spent on bread and 95% spent on wine.

A. What is true about the MU/P for bread and wine at this point? Explain how you know to increase the percentage spent on bread as a result of the values of MU/P for bread and wine. What happens to the difference between the MU/P for the two goods as you increase the amount spent on bread? What happens to utility as you increase the percentage spent on bread?

B. Continue to increase the percentage spent on bread until the values of MU/P are as close as possible and you have reached the highest utility for the given choice of leisure and work. What is true about the Marginal Utilities per dollar for bread and wine at that point? What is your value of utility? Is utility maximized at this point? Explain.

C. If utility is not maximized at this point, change the amount of time worked. Continue until you find the utility maximizing point. You might also have to change the percentage amount spent on bread and wine. What is true about the marginal utilities per dollar of all three goods (leisure, bread, and wine)? Compare your utility here to that in part B. Is utility higher in part C?

Activity 4: Utility Maximization using MU/P = MU/P
Consider Figure 53.

Figure 53: Consumption Options

Consumption Options

Savings: ○ Deposit of   [＿＿＿＿＿]
         ○ Withdrawal of [＿＿＿＿＿]

Leisure/Work Split: [50% / 50% ▾] (Leisure Hours 500, Work Hours 500)

Bread/Wine Split: [80% / 20% ▾] (80% of Expenditures for Bread, 20% for Wine

Expenditures and Utility

	Bread	Wine	Leisure
Units Consumed	600.00	150.00	500.00
Expenditures	$2,400.00	$600.00	
MU	1.90	3.10	.90
MU/P	.48	.78	.15

Wage Income:	$3,000.00
Expenditures:	$3,000.00
Utility:	2,312.53

Show the Budget Line and Indifference Curve graph.

Based on the MU/P in Figure 53, what strategy should the consumer employ in order to maximize utility? For example, should the consumer spend more on bread or wine? Should the consumer work more or less? Explain your answers.

Activity 5 **Advanced**. *Calculating Marginal Utility Mathematically*

Consider the utility function $U = (Bread^{0.6}) (Wine^{0.2}) (Time^{0.2})$. Calculate the utility from consuming 10 units of bread, 10 units of wine, and 60 hours of leisure (time). Now increase bread to 11. Recalculate the utility. What is the marginal utility of the 11th unit of bread? How about for the 12th unit of bread? Is the law of diminishing marginal utility supported in this case? Can you find a mathematical formula that would represent MU bread for all levels of bread?

Activity 6 **Advanced**. *Utility Maximization with Calculus*

The utility maximization problems in the game will differ depending on the utility function of your consumer. Let's consider one possible example, assuming that Joe, the consumer, has 100 hours of time in a period to delegate to work or leisure. Assume Joe works 50 hours for $10 per hour. Assume the price of bread is $30 and the price of wine is $10. Assume Joe's utility function is: $U = (Bread^{0.6}) (Wine^{0.2}) (Time^{0.2})$. Find Joe's utility maximizing points of consumption for bread and wine, given the prices, income, and choice of leisure time.

2.2. UTILITY MAXIMIZATION (MRS = P_X/P_Y)

Some books call this concept "The Theory of Consumer Choice". Whatever it is called, the idea is that consumers want to get the most satisfaction that they can, given the income they have and prices they face. A measure of consumer satisfaction is called **utility**. Utility is defined as the total satisfaction an individual receives from consuming a particular amount of goods (sometimes called a bundle of goods). One way to represent possible tradeoffs in consumption is with an **indifference curve**. An indifference curve shows all the combinations of two goods that will yield the consumer the same amount of satisfaction (or utility). The name is easy to remember since the consumer is "indifferent" between all the points on an indifference curve, thus the consumer likes all the points on an indifference curve equally. As long as the consumer prefers both goods (this will be the case with the game), then you will give up some of good y to get more of good x, thus the indifference curve is downward sloping. Also, as long as the consumer prefers more of both goods, then a consumer gets more satisfaction on indifference curves that are higher (further from the origin) than those lower (closer to the origin).

The slope of the indifference curve is called **Marginal Rate of Substitution (MRS)**. MRS is defined as the amount of good y the consumer is willing to give up for an extra unit of good x and remain at the same level of satisfaction (or utility). With the exception of extreme examples (such as perfect complements and perfect substitutes), the slope of the indifference curve gets flatter as x increases. This is usually described as convex to the origin or bowed inward. The MRS changes along an indifference curve with the higher values of MRS at the left-hand tail of the curve and the lower values of MRS at the right-hand tail of the curve.

The goal of a consumer is to achieve the highest indifference curve they can, given the prices and income that they are faced with. A way of representing the income and prices that a consumer is constrained by is called a consumer's **budget line**. A budget line shows all the possible combinations of two goods the consumer can afford to buy, with given prices and income. For example, if a consumer spends all his or her income on two goods, X and Y, and the price of good X is $5, the price of good Y is $2 and the consumer has $50 to spend, then Table 15 reflects some of the points on the consumer's budget line.

Table 15

Quantity of good X	Quantity of good Y
10	0
8	5
6	10
4	15
2	20
0	25

Graphing these points, with quantity of good X on the X axis and quantity of good Y on the Y axis, will yield a downward sloping graph with a slope of -2.5. The slope of the budget line is equal to the ratio of the prices, – Px/Py. In order to afford to buy one more unit of good X, I'd have to buy 2.5 units less of good Y. That is because good X is 2.5 times more expensive than good Y. Thus, you can hopefully see that the slope of the budget constraint depends on the ratio of the prices of the goods, even though the units on the X and Y axis are quantities of the good.

A consumer's optimal choices will involve selecting the amount of two goods he or she should consume that will get to the highest indifference curve, given the budget line. Graphically, given a particular budget line, the consumer will choose the point on the indifference curve where the indifference curve is tangent to the budget line. Tangent implies the slopes of the budget line and indifference curve are equal. Thus, at the utility maximizing point (or consumer equilibrium or optimum), the MRS = Px/Py. At this point, we know the consumer is on the highest indifference curve he or she can be on, given the budget line. Thus, the consumer has reached the highest level of utility. In Figure 54, the consumer is maximizing his or her utility. At the utility maximizing point, he or she is consuming 45 units of bread and 39 units of wine. The consumer could not reach a higher indifference curve without more income to spend or a change in the price ratio of the goods.

Figure 54: Budget Line and Indifference Curve Graph

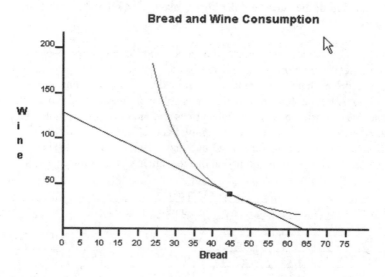

Bread and Wine Consumption

In the game, the consumer chooses between three goods: leisure, and two other goods that are produced by firms, such as bread and wine. The optimum rule still follows where the $MRS_{lw} = Price_w/Price_l$ and $MRS_{lb} = Price_b/Price_l$ and $MRS_{bw} = Price_w/Price_b$, where b stands for bread, w stands for wine, and l stands for leisure. In situations where the consumer's utility is not maximized, the MRS might be either larger or smaller than the price ratio. It is probably best to look at picture to see how the consumer could adjust his or her consumption of the goods in order to get to a higher indifference curve.

Activity 1: Points on a budget line

Click on the link to the Consumer Worksheet Page from the top navigation bar. Set the wage rate equal to 10, the price of bread equal to 8 and the price of wine equal to 5. Let's assume you begin with 100 hours of leisure. Under Consumption Options, choose to split leisure and work by choosing to spend 60 % of your time on leisure and 40 % of your time working. Begin with 5% spent on bread and 95% spent on wine. Increase the percentage spent on bread until you have reached the highest utility for the given choice of leisure and work. (Since you are holding leisure time constant, the MRS for leisure and bread and leisure and wine will not equal their relative prices here.) Show that the amount of bread and amount of wine that you should buy are on the budget line.

Activity 2: Shifts in Budget Lines

Click on the link to the Consumer Worksheet Page from the top navigation bar. Set the wage rate equal to 10, the price of bread equal to 8 and the price of wine equal to 5. Let's assume you begin with 100 hours of leisure. Under Consumption Options, choose to split leisure and work by choosing to spend 60 % of your time on leisure and 40 % of your time working. Begin with 5% spent on bread and 95% spent on wine.

- A. What is your income? Graph the consumer's budget line for the income and prices. (You may check your answer—in terms of the endpoints—by clicking on "Show" link from "Show the Budget Line and Indifference Curve graph" option at the bottom of the Consumer Worksheet Page. Recall that this link will not appear unless you have entered prices in the text boxes at the top of the Consumer Worksheet. Choose the graph for bread and wine to verify your answer.)

- B. Now change the amount of leisure to 40 (and the amount of work to 60 hours). On your same graph as in part A, graph the consumer's new budget line. What has happened to the budget line? Explain. (You may check your answer—in terms of the endpoints—as you did in part A. above.)

Activity 3: MRS = Px/Py
Click on the link to the Consumer Worksheet Page. Set the prices of the two goods and the wage rate equal to $5. Under Consumption Options, choose to split leisure and work by choosing to leisure for 80 hours and work for 20 hours. Begin with 5% spent on bread and 95% spent on wine.

A.   What is true about the MRS for bread and wine compared to the relative price of bread and wine? Explain how you know to increase the percentage spent on bread as a result of the comparison of the MRS of bread for wine to its relative price.

B.   What happens to the difference between the MRS of bread and wine to its relative price as you increase the amount spent on bread? What happens to the value of utility as you increase the percentage spent on bread?

C.   Continue to increase the percentage spent on bread until the MRS of bread and wine is as close as possible to the relative price and you have reached the highest utility for the given choice of leisure and work. Click on the "Show" link in the "Show Budget Line and Indifference Curve graph" option at the bottom of the Consumer Worksheet. Choose the graph for bread and wine. What is true about the indifference curve and budget line at this point?

D.   If utility is not maximized at this point, change the amount of time worked. Continue until you find the utility maximizing point. You might also have to change the percentage amount spent on bread and wine. What is true about the MRS of wine and bread, MRS of leisure and bread, and the MRS of leisure and wine compared to the relative price ratio? Look at the graphs for all three comparisons (leisure and bread, leisure and wine, wine and bread). Has your consumer now maximized utility? What is true for each graph?

Activity 4: Moving towards the optimal solution
Consider Figure 55. In this graph, the consumer is consuming 58 units of bread and 13 units of wine. That point is represented by the black box where the indifference curve intersects the budget line. Let's call that point, point A.

Figure 55: Budget Line and Indifference Curve Graph

Bread and Wine Consumption

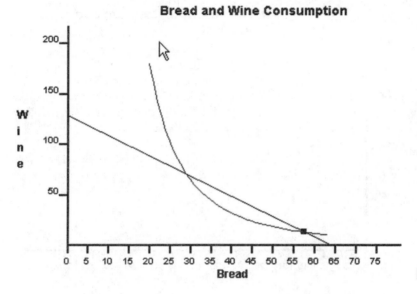

A. Is the consumer currently maximizing utility at point A? Why or why not?
B. What is true about MRS and the price ratio of price of bread to price of wine at point A?
C. Describe what the consumer might do in order to maximize utility. On the graph above, draw in a possible point where the consumer might be maximizing utility. Show the consumer maximizing utility at that point.
D. Has the consumer bought more or less bread at the utility maximizing point compared to point A? Has the consumer bought more or less wine at the utility maximizing point compared to point A?

Activity 5: Moving towards the optimal solution

Consider Figure 56. In this graph, the consumer is currently consuming 26 units of bread and 77 units of wine. That point is represented by the black box where the indifference curve intersects the budget line. Let's call that point, point A.

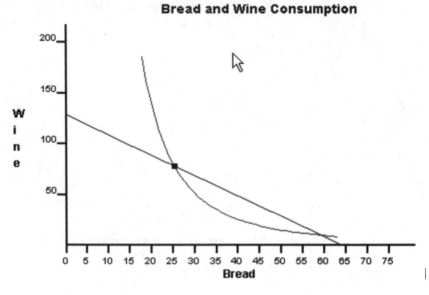

Figure 56: Budget Line and Indifference Curve Graph

Bread and Wine Consumption

A. Is the consumer currently maximizing utility at point A? Why or why not?
B. What is true about MRS and the price ratio of price of bread to price of wine at point A?
C. Describe what the consumer might do in order to maximize utility. On the graph above, draw in a possible point where the consumer might be maximizing utility. Show the consumer maximizing utility at that point.
D. Has the consumer bought more or less bread at the utility maximizing point compared to point A? Has the consumer bought more or less wine at the utility maximizing point compared to point A?

*Activity 6 **Advanced**. Graphing an Indifference Curve*
Consider the utility function $U = XY$, where X and Y are two goods. Plot the indifference curve for a utility level equal to 20 using at least 4 points. Is your indifference curve downward sloping? Does your indifference curve have a convex (or bowed inward) shape?

*Activity 7 **Advanced**. Utility Maximization with Calculus*
The utility maximization problems in the game will differ depending on the utility function of your consumer. Let's consider one possible example,

assuming that Joe, the consumer, has 100 hours of time in a period to delegate to work or leisure. Assume Joe works 50 hours for $10 per hour. Assume the price of bread is $30 and the price of wine is $10. Assume Joe's utility function is: U = (Bread$^{0.6}$) (Wine$^{0.2}$) (Time$^{0.2}$). Find Joe's utility maximizing points of consumption for bread and wine, given the prices, income, and choice of leisure time.

3. Labor Supply

The market for labor is such that consumers are suppliers of labor and firms are the demanders of labor. In Adam's market, your consumer supplies labor to firms. An individual consumer's supply curve for labor is made up of all the utility maximizing points between income and leisure. Typically the consumer's supply curve for labor is upward sloping. Each point represents the amount of hours a consumer is willing to work at each wage rate. As the wage rate increases, we are willing to work more hours. Sometimes, an individual's supply curve for labor can begin to bend backward at very high wages. At some point, as wages increase, we might actually choose to work less.

This result might seem odd, but is not. When the wage rate changes, the total effect of that wage change is broken down into two different parts. The **substitution effect** allows the consumer to consider the effect of the wage rate change on his or her behavior without considering the actual change in income that might result in that wage change. Thus, the consumer only considers the relative change in the price of work versus the price of leisure. The substitution effect causes consumers to substitute into the relatively cheaper "good". Thus, if the wage rate increases, it becomes more expensive to spend time on leisure and the substitution effect part of your response would lead you to consume less leisure and work more. The **income effect** refers to the consumer's response to the possible change in income as a result of the wage change. As long as leisure is a **normal good** (we consume more leisure as income increases), then as the wage rate increases and income increases for each hour worked, then the income effect would cause the consumer to consume more leisure and work less.

As you can see, there is a conflict here. When the wage rate increases, the substitution effect causes the consumer to consume less leisure, but the income effect causes the consumer to consume more leisure. The total effect is a sum of both the substitution effect and the income effect. Thus, for an increase in wages, the total effect could result in one of three outcomes: the consumer chooses to use more time for leisure (work less) if the income effect is bigger than the substitution effect, the consumer chooses to use less leisure (work more) if the substitution effect is bigger than the income effect, or to consume the same amount of leisure as before the wage change (work the same) if the income effect and substitution effect are the same size. So you can see that a backwards bending supply curve for labor just means that for the low level of wages, the substitution effect is bigger than the income effect and then for the backward bending part of the supply curve, the income effect is bigger than the substitution effect.

Activity 1: Determining your consumer's labor supply function
Click on the link to the Consumer Worksheet from the top navigation bar. In the table labeled "Prices" enter a price of 5 for bread, 7 for wine, and 10 for wage rate. Under "Consumer Options", find the leisure/work split and wine/bread split that will maximize utility.

A. How many hours are you willing to work at a wage rate of $10?

B. On a graph with wage rate on the Y axis and hours of labor on the X axis, graph the point that reflects your utility maximizing result from part A above.

C. In the table labeled "Prices", change the wage rate to 15, keeping the price of wine and bread constant. Under "Consumer Options", find the utility maximizing point of leisure, bread consumption, and wine consumption with the new wage rate. How many hours are you willing to work at a wage rate of $15?

D. On your graph in part B, graph the point that reflects your utility maximizing result from part C above.

E. In the table labeled "Prices", change the wage rate to 20, keeping the price of wine and bread constant. Under "Consumer Options", find the utility maximizing point of leisure, bread consumption, and wine consumption with the new wage rate. How many hours are you willing to work at a wage rate of $20?

F. On your graph in part B, graph the point that reflects your utility maximizing result from part E above.

G. What can you say about the shape of the supply curve for labor? Is it upward sloping? Is it vertical? Do you think the supply curve for labor that you graphed is a reasonable representation as to how consumers might respond to wage changes? Explain your answers.

Activity 2: Substitution and Income Effects
In activity 1, we increased the wage rate. As the wage rate increased, you were able to assess the total effect. Given your answers in activity 1, discuss the direction of both the income and substitution effect of the wage increase. What has to be true about the relative sizes of the income and substitution effect given the total effect of the wage increase in activity 1?

4. Profit-maximizing level of output, short run

Economists distinguish between the short run and long run in the following way: in the short run there is at least one fixed input. In the long run, all inputs are variable. Thus, in the short run, we have both fixed inputs and variable inputs. The costs associated with each specific type of input are appropriately called **Variable Costs (VC) and Fixed Costs (FC)**. We refer to **total costs (TC)** as the sum of VC + FC. We typically assume that firms produce the level of output in order to maximize profit. Profits are defined as **Total Revenue (TR) – Total Costs (TC)**. Total Revenue is defined as the total amount of receipts the firm would receive from selling a certain amount of output. TR is calculated as price times quantity.

The additional revenue the firm receives from producing an additional unit of output is called **Marginal Revenue (MR)** and is defined as the change in total revenue divided by the change in output (Q). The additional cost of producing an additional unit of output is called **Marginal Cost (MC)** and is defined as the change in total cost divided by the change in output (Q). Table 16 shows how to calculate MC and MR. The columns marked in bold have been calculated.

Table 16

Output	Price	TR	MR	VC	FC	TC	MC	Profit
0	**10**	**0**	——	**0**	**100**	**100**	——	-100
25	**10**	**250**	250/25 = 10	**200**	**100**	**300**	200/25 = 8	-50
60	**10**	**600**	350/35 = 10	**400**	**100**	**500**	200/35 = 5.71	100
90	**10**	**900**	300/30 = 10	**600**	**100**	**700**	200/30 = 6.67	200
110	**10**	1100	200/20 = 10	**800**	**100**	**900**	200/20 = 10	200
120	**10**	1200	100/10 = 10	**1000**	**100**	**1100**	200/10 = 20	100

The Total Revenue (TR) is calculated as Price times Output. In this example, it is assumed the price stays the same no matter how many units are sold. This is similar to the table in Adam's market, where you will specify the price of output. Marginal Revenue (MR) is calculated as the change in total revenue divided by the change in output. Note that FC is the same for all levels of output. This would represent the cost of all the firm's fixed inputs. Notice that VC varies with output. If the firm is not producing any output, then VC is equal to 0. Marginal Cost (MC) is calculated as the change in total cost divided by the change in output. Notice that since FC is constant, the change in TC is the same as the change in VC, so MC could equally be computed using the formula change in VC divided by the change in output.

In order to maximize profit, the firm thinks on the margin. For each additional unit of output, it compares the MR to the MC. If the MR is bigger than the MC, then the firm will produce that level of output and profits will increase. If the MR < MC, the firm will not choose to produce that level of output since profits would fall at that point. Thus, profits are maximized where MR = MC. In the table above, profits would be maximized at an output level of 110, where profits equal 200. Any point beyond that, profits would fall. Notice that at the output level of 110, MR = MC and profits to the firm are at their highest (200). If the firm continues to produce more output beyond that point, MR < MC, and profits fall to 100.

Activity 1: Fixed Inputs and Variable Inputs
Click on the link to the Firm Worksheet from the top navigation bar. In the ticker at the bottom of the page, you can see the amount of cash and the amount of inputs used this period. Which input(s) represent the variable input? Which input(s) represent the fixed input(s)?

Activity 2: Calculating Variable Costs (VC) and Total Revenue (TR)
Click on the link to the Firm Worksheet from the top navigation bar. Find the area called "Set Values". Enter the value for capital that you have (shown in the ticker under "Inputs Used This Period"). Assume the wage rate is 10 and your output price is 5. Click on the button marked "Update Table and Graphs Below". View the resulting values in terms of output (the default radio button). Numbers will appear in the table below that button. The first column is "Labor", the amount of labor hired by your firm. The second column is "Output", the amount of product your firm can produce hiring that much labor (given the amount of capital you set).
A. Calculate TR (Total Revenue) for the first three rows and compare your answer with the table. How is TR calculated?
B. Calculate VC (Variable Costs) for the first three rows and compare your answer with the table. How is VC calculated?

Activity 3: Calculating Marginal Cost (MC) and Marginal Revenue (MR)
Click on the link to the Firm Worksheet from the top navigation bar. Find the area called "Set Values". Enter the value for capital that you have (shown in the ticker under "Inputs Used This Period"). Assume the wage rate is 10 and your output price is 5. Click on the button marked "Update Table and Graphs Below". Numbers will appear in the table below that button. View the resulting values in terms of output (the default radio button).
A. Calculate MR (Marginal Revenue) for the first three rows and compare your answer with the table. How is MR calculated?
B. Calculate MC (Marginal Cost) for the first three rows and compare your answer with the table. How is MC calculated?

Activity 4: Finding Profit Maximizing Level of Output

Click on the link to the firm worksheet. Find the area called "Set Values". Enter the value for capital that you have (shown in the ticker under "Inputs Used This Period"). Assume the wage rate is 10 and your output price is 5. Click on the button marked "Update Table and Graphs Below." Numbers will appear in the table below that button. View the resulting values in terms of output (the default radio button).

 A. Using MR and MC, find the level of output where profits are maximized. What is true about MR and MC at this level of output?

 B. In the table, there is a column labeled "TR-VC". Since the firm does not pay for the capital allocated to it, the firm essentially has no FC. Thus, TC = VC and so, profits = TR – VC. Verify that your firm's profits are maximized at the output level chosen in part A above. Record the level of profits the firm earns at the profit maximizing level.

 C. How much labor should the firm hire in order to produce the profit maximizing level of output?

Activity 5: Decreases in Output Price

Click on the link to the Firm Worksheet from the top navigation bar. Find the area called "Set Values". Enter the value for capital that you have (shown in the ticker under "Inputs Used This Period"). Assume the wage rate is 10 and your output price is 4. Click on the button marked "Update Table and Graphs Below". Numbers will appear in the table below that button. View the resulting values in terms of output (the default radio button).

 A. The price of output is lower in this example than in activity 4. What would you expect to happen to the amount of output produced? What would you expect to happen to the firm's profits?

 B. Using MR and MC, find the level of output where profits are maximized. Record the level of profits the firm earns at the profit maximizing level.

 C. Compare the level of output produced and the profits earned to your answer in activity 4. Were your predictions from part A right?

Activity 6: Increases in Output Price

Click on the link to the Firm Worksheet from the top navigation bar. Find the area called "Set Values". Enter the value for capital that you have (shown in the ticker under "Inputs Used This Period"). Assume the wage rate is 10 and your output price is 8. Click on the button marked "Update Table and Graphs Below". Numbers will appear in the table below that button. View the resulting values in terms of output (the default radio button).

 A. The price of output is higher in this example than in activity 4 (and 5). What would you expect to happen to the amount of output produced? What would you expect to happen to the firm's profits?

B. Using MR and MC, find the level of output where profits are maximized. Record the level of profits the firm earns at the profit maximizing level.
C. Compare the level of output produced and the profits earned to your answer in activity 4. Were your predictions from part A right?

Activity 7: Finding Profit Maximizing Amount of Output
Consider Figure 57, which shows the results of the "Output, Costs and Revenues with Different Amounts of Labor" Table from the firm worksheet page of Adam's market.

Figure 57: Firm Worksheet In Terms of Output

Adam's Market Firm Worksheet

Labor Worksheet   Capital Worksheet

Recent Offer History

	Last Four Purchases				Lowest Four Offers Available			
Wage Rate	6.0	6.0	6.0	6.0	6.0	6.0	N/A	N/A
Output Price (Bread)	4.0	3.8	3.8	3.8	3.5	3.8	4.0	4.0

Refresh List

Set Values
Capital Stock: 14.4   Wage Price: 6   Output Price: 4

Update Table and Graphs Below

View Resulting Values with Various Amounts of Labor
◉ In Terms of Output ○ In Terms of Labor

Labor	Output	TR	VC	AVC	MC	MR	TR-VC
147	460.09	1,840.35	882.00	1.92	3.81	4.00	958.35
150	464.76	1,859.03	900.00	1.94	3.85	4.00	959.03
153	469.38	1,877.53	918.00	1.96	3.89	4.00	959.53
156	473.96	1,895.85	936.00	1.97	3.93	4.00	959.85
159	478.50	1,913.99	954.00	1.99	3.97	4.00	959.99
162	482.99	1,931.96	972.00	2.01	4.01	4.00	959.96
165	487.44	1,949.77	990.00	2.03	4.04	4.00	959.77
168	491.85	1,967.41	1,008.00	2.05	4.08	4.00	959.41

A. What is the level of output that maximizes profit?
B. Using the relationship between MR and MC, explain why the firm should not produce 491.85 units of output.
C. Using the relationship between MR and MC, explain why the firm should produce more than 469.38 units of output.
D. How many units of labor should the firm hire in order to produce the profit maximizing level of output? How much will it cost the firm to hire the profit maximizing amount of labor?

*Activity 8 **Advanced**. Assume the firm sells output for $8.02 per unit. The cost of production can be found with the equation: TC = .04Q² + .02Q.*

    A.   What is the marginal revenue of the firm?

    B.   Solve for the marginal cost of the firm.

    C.   What is the profit maximizing level of output the firm should produce? Calculate profits at the profit maximizing level of output.

5. Profit-maximizing level of employment, short run

The problem of profit maximization can be examined in terms of the output produced to maximize profits, or similarly, in terms of the labor hired (that will then produce the profit maximizing level of output). The decision, in the end, will yield the same result. A firm's demand for labor is called the Marginal Revenue Product (MRP) of labor. This is defined as the additional revenue that the firm earns from hiring an additional unit of labor. There are two steps for the firm to earn additional revenue from hiring additional labor. First, the firm hires the labor and the labor makes additional product. Then, the firm sells the additional product to earn the additional revenue. Thus, MRP is calculated as MP_L times MR, where MP_L is the marginal product of labor (the additional output from hiring an additional unit of labor) and MR is the marginal revenue (the additional revenue earned from selling an additional unit of output). Table 17 shows how MRP of labor is calculated.

Table 17

Labor (L)	Output	Marginal Product (MP)	**Marginal Revenue (MR)**	MRP
0	0	—-	10	—
1	20	20	10	200
2	50	30	10	300
3	70	20	10	200

The columns in bold were calculated. The columns for Labor, Output, and Marginal Revenue (MR) were given. MP_L is calculated as the change in output divided by the change in labor. Since the MR is constant here, we can assume that the output market is perfectly competitive and MR is equal to the price of output. MRP is calculated as MP_L times the MR.

In the case of the game, the wage rate is given and firms act as wage takers. Thus, the wage represents the additional cost resulting from hiring an additional worker.

The firm will maximize profits when the MRP is equal to the wage rate. If the MRP is greater than the wage rate, then the firm could earn more profits by continuing to hire labor. If the MRP is less than the wage rate, then the firm's profits will fall by hiring that additional worker. Only when the MRP = wage rate will the firm be maximizing its profit.

Activity 1: Calculating Marginal Product of Labor (MP)

Click on the link to the Firm Worksheet from the top navigation bar. Find the area called "Set Values". Enter the value for capital that you have (shown in the ticker under "Inputs Used This Period"). Assume the wage rate is 10 and your output price is 5. Click on the button marked "Update Table and Graphs Below". Numbers will appear in the table below that button. Click the radio button to view the resulting values in terms of labor. The first column is "Labor", the amount of labor hired by your firm. The second column is "Output", the amount of product your firm can produce hiring that much labor (given the amount of capital you set).

    A.   Calculate MP (Marginal Product of Labor) for the first three rows and compare your results with the table. How is MP calculated?

    B.   What does MR equal in this case? Explain.

Activity 2: Calculating Marginal Revenue Product (MRP)

Click on the link to the Firm Worksheet from the top navigation bar. Find the area called "Set Values". Enter the value for capital that you have (shown in the ticker under "Inputs Used This Period"). Assume the wage rate is 10 and your output price is 5. Click on the button marked "Update Table and Graphs Below." Numbers will appear in the table below that button. Click the radio button to view the resulting values in terms of labor. Use the numbers in the table to help you calculate MRP (Marginal Revenue Product of Labor) for the first three rows. Compare your results with the values in the table. How is MRP calculated?

Activity 3: Finding Profit Maximizing Level of Labor

Click on the link to the Firm Worksheet from the top navigation bar. Find the area called "Set Values". Enter the value for capital that you have (shown in the ticker under "Inputs Used This Period"). Assume the wage rate is 10 and your output price is 5. Click on the button marked "Update Table and Graphs Below". Numbers will appear in the table below that button. Click the radio button to view the resulting values in terms of labor.

    A.   Using MRP and wage, find the level of labor where profits are maximized. What is true about MRP and the wage at this level of labor?

    B.   In the table, there is a column labeled "TR-VC." Since the firm does not pay for the capital allocated to it, the firm essentially has no FC. Thus, TC = VC and so, profits = TR – VC. Verify that your firm's profits are maximized at the amount of labor chosen in part A above. Record the level of profits the firm earns at the profit maximizing level.

C. How much output does the firm produce when it hires the profit maximizing level of labor?

D. Now, click on the radio button to view the table in terms of output. Find the level of output from your answer in part C. What is true about MR and MC at that level of output?

Activity 4: Decreases in the Wage Rate

Click on the link to the Firm Worksheet from the top navigation bar. Find the area called "Set Values". Enter the value for capital that you have (shown in the ticker under "Inputs Used This Period"). Assume the wage rate is 7 and your output price is 5. Click on the button marked "Update Table and Graphs Below". Numbers will appear in the table below that button. Click the radio button to view the resulting values in terms of labor.

A. The wage rate is lower in this example than in activity 3. What would you expect to happen to the amount of labor hired as the wage rate falls? What would you expect to happen to the firm's profits?

B. Using MRP and wage, find the quantity of labor where profits are maximized. Record the level of profits the firm earns at the profit maximizing level.

C. Compare the level of labor hired and the profits earned to your answer in activity 3. Were your predictions from part A correct?

Activity 5: Increases in the Wage Rate

Click on the link to the Firm Worksheet from the top navigation bar. Find the area called "Set Values". Enter the value for capital that you have (shown in the ticker under "Inputs Used This Period"). Assume the wage rate is 12 and your output price is 5. Click on the button marked "Update Table and Graphs Below". Numbers will appear in the table below that button. Click the radio button to view the resulting values in terms of labor.

A. The wage rate is higher in this example than in activity 3 (and 4). What would you expect to happen to the amount of labor hired as the wage rate falls? What would you expect to happen to the firm's profits?

B. Using MRP and wage, find the level of labor where profits are maximized. Record the level of profits the firm earns at the profit maximizing level.

C. Compare the level of labor hired and the profits earned to your answer in activity 3. Were your predictions from part A correct?

Activity 6: Finding the Profit Maximizing Amount of Labor

In Section 4, Activity 7, you were given a table and asked to find the profit maximizing level of output. The same capital, wage and output information was used to produce what is shown in Figure 58.

Figure 58: Firm's Worksheet in Terms of Labor

Adam's Market Firm Worksheet

Labor Worksheet   Capital Worksheet

Recent Offer History

	Last Four Purchases				Lowest Four Offers Available			
Wage Rate	6.0	6.0	6.0	6.0	6.0	6.0	N/A	N/A
Output Price (Bread)	4.0	3.8	3.8	3.8	3.5	3.8	4.0	4.0

Refresh List

Set Values

Capital Stock: 14.4   Wage Price: 6   Output Price: 4

Update Table and Graphs Below

View Resulting Values with Various Amounts of Labor

○ In Terms of Output ◉ In Terms of Labor

Labor	Output	MP	MR	MRP	Wage	TR-VC
147	460.09	1.57	4.00	6.29	6.00	958.35
150	464.76	1.56	4.00	6.23	6.00	959.03
153	469.38	1.54	4.00	6.17	6.00	959.53
156	473.96	1.53	4.00	6.11	6.00	959.85
159	478.50	1.51	4.00	6.05	6.00	959.99
162	482.99	1.50	4.00	5.99	6.00	959.96
165	487.44	1.48	4.00	5.94	6.00	959.77
168	491.85	1.47	4.00	5.88	6.00	959.41

A. What is the level of labor that should be hired to maximize profit?
B. Using the relationship between MRP and wage explain why the firm should not hire 168 units of labor.
C. Using the relationship between MRP and wage, explain why the firm should hire more than 150 units of labor.
D. How much output does the firm produce when it hires the profit maximizing level of labor? What would you expect to be true about MR and MC at this output level?
E. Compare your answer in part D above to that from activity 7, part A., in section 4 above. Explain the similarities of the two answers and tables.

*Activity 7 **Advanced**. Consider the production function $Q = L^{1/2}K^{1/2}$.*
Assume the amount of capital is fixed at 36 units. Assume the wage rate
is $10 and the price of output is $10.

    A.   Calculate the firm's marginal product of labor (MP_L).

    B.   Calculate the firm's MRP curve.

    C.   Find the profit maximizing amount of labor the firm should hire. What level of output will maximize profits?

    D.   Calculate TR for the firm at the profit maximizing level of output. Calculate VC of producing the profit maximizing level of output. Calculate the firm's profits (if we assume the cost of capital to the firm was zero).

6. Depreciation

To produce goods firms use capital (plants and equipment). Unfortunately, plants and equipment do not last forever. Equipment might be damaged while producing output or become obsolete. Economists refer to the loss in value of a firm's capital as depreciation. Economists include depreciation as one of the implicit costs of producing output.

In Adam's Market your capital stock does not depreciate in the short run. In the long run (when you are able to make capital purchases), your capital stock will depreciate at the end of each period at some constant percentage chosen by your instructor. In addition, the value of your inventory will decrease at the end of each period as well. This reflects the routine charge for the percentage of goods in the inventory that might spoil if they are not consumed in the current period.

To see the effects of depreciation, call up the firm's worksheet and click on the link to the Capital Worksheet (you will only be able to do this if it is possible to purchase capital). As shown in Figure 59, the screen will display the number of units of capital your firm will have with no additional purchases of capital. In this case the depreciation rate is 10 percent and the initial capital stock is 11.52 units (it is listed as "Actual Capital"). Assuming that capital purchases were able to be made in period 2 (for use in period 3), but that no new capital was purchased, the capital stock will fall to 10.37 in the next period (10.37 = 11.52 − (0.1)(11.52)).

Figure 59: Capital Worksheet (on following page)

View Values

Actual (non-worksheet) Capital Stock: 11.52	Depreciation Rate: 10.0%	Current Price for Capital:

Set Values

Additional Capital Purchase: 2   Output Price: 5

Labor per Period: 30   Discount Rate: 0 %

[Update Table Below]

View Net Present Value of New Capital

Period	Capital without Additional Purchase	Capital with Additional Purchase	Output Change	Revenue Change	Present Value of Revenue Change
3	10.37	12.37	16.26	81.30	81.30
4	9.33	11.13	15.43	77.13	77.13
5	8.40	10.02	14.63	73.17	73.17
6	7.56	9.02	13.88	69.42	69.42

Present Value of Additional Revenue: 301.03
Cost of Additional Capital: 58.11
Net Present Value: 242.92

Example

Assume that you have 100 units of capital at the start of period 1 and that capital can be bought in period 1, so that depreciation begins immediately. If the depreciation rate is 10%, how much capital would you have at the start of (1) period 2, and (2) period 3?

Solutions

1. At the end of period 1, 10 units of capital will be lost (10% of 100 units). This means that the amount of capital at the beginning of period 2 = 100 – 10 = **90 units**.
2. At the end of period 2, 9 units of capital will be lost (10% of 90 units). This means that the amount of capital at the beginning of period 3 = 90 – 9 = **81 units**

Activity 1

Assume your capital stock is 100 units of capital at the start of period 1 and that capital can be bought in period 1, so that depreciation begins immediately. If the depreciation rate is 5 percent, how much capital would you have at the start of (A) period 2, and (B) period 3?

Activity 2
Assume you have 200 units of output in inventory at the start of period 5. If you do not sell any output during the period and the depreciation rate for inventory is 20 percent, how many units of output would you have at the start of the next period?

7. Profit-maximizing level of capital, long-run

As you recall, the short run is defined as the situation when at least one input is fixed. In the case of Adam's market, capital is the fixed input. However, at some point in the game your firm will have the opportunity to purchase capital for use in future periods. In most cases, as discussed in the previous section, your professor will have set capital to depreciate over time. Once your firm has purchased capital, it will have some portion of that capital to use for the remainder of the game. The decision of whether to produce capital is one in which the additional costs of buying additional capital must be compared to the additional revenue the firm could earn from buying capital. If the additional costs are greater than the additional revenue the firm would earn by purchasing additional capital, then the firm should not buy capital. However, if the additional revenue the firm gets from purchasing an additional unit of capital is greater than the additional cost of buying the capital, then the firm should buy the capital.

In the game, the Capital Worksheet link accessible from the Firm Worksheet will help your firm decide whether to purchase capital and how much capital to purchase. In order to understand the Capital Worksheet, you must understand the concept of **Present Value**. Present value is defined as the value, in today's dollars, of what you will receive at a specific date in the future.

In terms of the example above, each period that you have additional capital, your firm will be able to produce more output with the same amount of labor hired and earn additional revenue. The sum of the additional revenue over every period would tell us the total additional revenue from purchasing capital. However, since your firm will not receive those revenues until the future, it needs to be **discounted** in terms of what it is worth today. Most likely, your professor might set the discount rate to zero, so that the sum of the additional revenues will simply equal the present value of the additional revenues. In the Capital Worksheet, you are able to choose the discount rate you want to use or your professor might recommend using a specific rate. Whatever choice for the discount rate, the table will tell you the Present Value (PV) of the change in revenue. Just remember this is basically what the additional revenue from buying capital is worth to you in today's dollars (the period in which you are trying to decide whether or not to buy capital).

Once the PV of additional revenue is calculated, it is subtracted from the cost of the additional capital. This difference is called the **net present value**. If the net present value from a particular amount of capital is positive, then you should buy that capital. If the net present value from a particular amount of capital is negative, then it costs you more to buy the capital than you will earn in the future. You should not buy the capital. You should try to find the level of capital where the net present value is at its highest. This is the profit maximizing level of capital you should buy.

Activity 1: The Discount Rate

Click on the link to the Firm Worksheet. Click on the link for the Capital Worksheet. At the bottom of the page, you will see the table labeled "View Net Present Value of Capital." Under Set Values, choose additional capital purchase to be 6, output price to be 5, and labor per period to be 40. Initially choose the discount rate to be 0. Click on the button "Update Table Below."

A. What is the net present value of capital in this situation? Should your firm buy this capital?
B. Compare the "Revenue Change" column in the table to the "Present Value of Revenue Change."
C. With a calculator, add up the values of the "Revenue Change" column for all the periods. How does your calculation compare to the "Present Value of Additional Revenue" given at the bottom of the table?
D. Keeping capital purchased, output price, and labor per period all constant, change the discount rate to 5%. Click on the button "Update Table Below." Compare the "Revenue Change" column to the "Present Value of Revenue Change." How do they compare? Can you explain the difference between the two numbers?
E. What has happened to the value of "Present Value of Additional Revenue" compared to your answer in C?
F. In general, what would you say happens to the present value as the discount rate increases?

Activity 2: Reading the "New Present Value of Capital" Table

Consider Figure 60, which was generated from the Capital Worksheet accessed from the Firm Worksheet window. The depreciation rate of capital is 10%.

Figure 60: Capital Worksheet

Set Values

Additional Capital Purchase: [14]   Output Price: [4]

Labor per Period: [30]   Discount Rate: [0] %

[Update Table Below]

View Net Present Value of New Capital

Period	Capital without Additional Purchase	Capital with Additional Purchase	Output Change	Revenue Change	Present Value of Revenue Change
3	12.96	26.96	87.21	348.86	348.86
4	11.66	24.26	82.74	330.95	330.95
5	10.50	21.84	78.49	313.97	313.97
6	9.45	19.65	74.46	297.86	297.86

Present Value of Additional Revenue: 1291.64
Cost of Additional Capital: 406.76
Net Present Value: 884.88

The second column of the table shows the units of capital each period if no new capital were purchased. The third column of the table shows the units of capital that the firm would have each period if it purchases 14 units of capital in period 2. (Remember you choose to purchase capital in the period prior to when you will have it available to use.) The fourth column "Output Change" shows the additional output that could be made as a result of purchasing the additional 14 units of capital.

- A. Explain why the values in the "Output Change" column fall in each period, from period 3 to period 6.
- B. Explain how the "Revenue Change" column is calculated in this example.
- C. Should this firm buy 14 units of capital in period 2? Explain why or why not.
- D. How will you determine whether the firm should buy 16 units of capital rather than 14?

Activity 3: Increases in output price on the capital decision
Consider Figure 61.

Figure 61

Additional Capital Purchase: 14   Output Price: 6

Labor per Period: 30   Discount Rate: 0   %

Update Table Below

View Net Present Value of New Capital

Period	Capital without Additional Purchase	Capital with Additional Purchase	Output Change	Revenue Change	Present Value of Revenue Change
3	12.96	26.96	87.21	523.28	523.28
4	11.66	24.26	82.74	496.43	496.43
5	10.50	21.84	78.49	470.96	470.96
6	9.45	19.65	74.46	446.79	446.79

Present Value of Additional Revenue: 1937.46
Cost of Additional Capital: 406.76
Net Present Value: 1530.70

A. Figure 61 is similar to the table in activity 2. In this table, the output price has increased from $4 to $6. Thinking about how the capital decision is determined, what would you think would be the likely effect of an increase in the output price in terms of amount of capital purchased this period?
B. In what way does the table above support your argument? Explain.

Activity 4: Decreases in output price on the capital decision
What would you think would be the likely effect of a decrease in the output price in terms of the amount of capital purchased in a given period? Explain.

Activity 5: Finding the profit maximizing level of capital to purchase
Click on the link to the firm worksheet window from the top navigation bar. Click on the link for the Capital Worksheet. Under the section "Set Values," enter an output price of $5, labor per period of 40 and a discount rate of 0. Begin with 2 units of Additional Capital Purchased. Click on the button "Update Table Below."

A. Assess whether your firm should purchase 2 additional units of capital. Continue to increase the additional capital purchased and update the table until you find the level of capital the firm should buy this period.
B. How much capital should the firm buy this period? Let's call this level of capital, K*.

C. Set the level of capital to 2 units lower than K*. Compare the net present value from this level of capital to the net present value from K*. How do they compare?

D. Set the level of capital to 2 units higher than K*. Compare the net present value from this level of capital to the net present value from K*. How do they compare?

E. Using the evidence above, justify your choice of K*.

Activity 6: The impact on the price of output of increases in capital

One of the main factors in determining the present value of additional revenue is the price of the product. As we learned in activity 3, increases in the price of output will generally cause an increase in the amount of capital bought. On the other hand, we learned in activity 4 that a decrease in the output price can cause a decrease in the amount of capital bought. When making our capital decision, we are asked to enter a price for the product. It is implied, from the table, that the price of the product will remain constant over time.

A. Do you think the assumption about the stability of the price of output is realistic? Explain.

B. Assume period 3 is the first period in which capital is able to be purchased. What do you think might happen to prices of output during period 4? Justify your answer.

C. Will this change in the price of output make your capital purchase have a higher present value or lower present value? Explain.

D. What does this potential change in present value (caused by the change in the price of output) imply about the profit maximizing level of capital purchased in period 3? Did you over buy or under buy capital?

8. Entry and Exit of Firms

Your professor might choose to give firms the option to change industries at some point in the game. The mechanical process to do so is simple. From the Firm Actions page, simply click on the "Change Industry" link. Choose the new industry in which you want to participate and then press the button labeled "Change Industry".

The decision about whether or not to change industries is not as simple. There is no table that will help you make the definite answer. You must use your knowledge of economics and the information you have to come to the most informed decision that you can.

Activity 1: Identifying Industries with Overproduction of Output

Click on the link to the Firm Graphs page from the left navigation panel. From the dropdown menu, choose the "Current Inventories" graph. Given this information alone, is there an industry that might be attractive to enter? Explain how you might determine which industry to enter.

Activity 2: Identifying Industries with High Profits
Click on the link to the Firm Graphs page from the left navigation panel. From the dropdown menu, choose the "Total Profit by Industry" graph and compare the profits of your industry to the profits of the other industries in the game.

Using the information in this graph, discuss which industry you might consider entering. If you are already a firm producing that good, discuss why others might choose to enter that industry. Is there additional information about profits you might find helpful in making your decision that is not shown in this graph?

Activity 3: Assessing your position within the industry
Before jumping in and automatically entering an industry that is doing well, you must consider your firm's individual performance in the industry. Click on the link to the Firm Graphs page from the left navigation panel. From the dropdown menu, choose the "Net Worth, My Group" graph.
   A.   How many firms are doing better than your firm? How many firms are doing worse than your firm? Use this information along with the information above to discuss whether you should enter the industry (or others should enter your industry).
   B.   Is there information about your consumer that you should consider prior to making a decision to enter a different industry?

Activity 4: The Impact of Entry into the Market
Before making the final decision, your firm must consider the impact that entry might have on the existing situation. What would be the most likely impact of entry on price of output, total output produced, and profits to firms?

Activity 5: The Impact of Exit out of the Market
Obviously if some firms change industries, there will be entry into the more attractive industry and exit out of the less attractive industry. What would be the most likely impact of exit on price of output, total output produced, and profits to firms?

9. Bond Market

Firms issue bonds in the primary market as a means to raise money, usually for capital financing. A bond is essentially a promise to pay a fixed amount of money at some future date. For example, if a firm needs $100,000 to buy new equipment, it might offer to sell a bond with a face value (FV) of $121,000 that matures in two periods for a price of $100,000. The date when the payment is made is called the maturity date. For example, a bond that matures in 20 years is called a 20-year bond.

Households buy bonds as a way of earning interest on their saving. By preserving part of their current income in this manner they defer today's consumption. However, holding bonds allows them to increase future consumption by reselling bonds from their portfolio and/or as the bonds mature. Firms also buy bonds issued by other firms as a way of earning interest on savings. Once issued, all of the outstanding bonds in the hands of the households and firms can be resold in the secondary market.

A bond that does not make any payment above the face value is a pure discount bond; it is always issued at a price less than its face value at the time of sale. The difference between the bond's selling price (SP) and the face value is the interest. For example, if a bond with a face value of $100,000 is sold at a discount price of $80,000, the interest to the buyer is $20,000. If the bond matures in one year, it would have an effective return rate of .25 (or 25%) that is equivalent to the bond yield [i.e., yield = (FV – SP) ÷ SP or = Interest ÷ SP]. In MarketSim, firms can only issue pure discount bonds.

In actual bond markets, most bonds also include a series of payments called coupon payments in addition to repayment of the principal. For example, the issuer of a 30-year bond with a face value of $100,000 might also promise to pay $5,000 for each of the 30 years plus the $100,000 at maturity. In this case, the series of coupon payments in each year must be incorporated in determining the bond price (or its present value) at the time of sale.

The principle of present value provides the theoretical basis for calculating the selling price of a bond in the current period. The present value is the value of a future payment or stream of payments in today's dollars. Thus, the selling price (SP) of a bond that promises to pay a certain face value (FV) with or without additional series of coupon payment (C) in each period during the maturity period is the present value (PV) of all the anticipated/promised future stream of payments.

For a pure discount bond, the general formula for calculating the present value (PV) of the stated FV of a bond can be summarized as:

$$PV = FV \div (1+ i)^t$$

As stated, 'i' is the quoted interest rate or yield, and 't' is the maturity period (t = 1, 2, …, 30 years). Since the PV is to be received at the end the 't' period, it is the highest price that one would pay in the current period to buy the bond.

For a coupon bond, the general formula for calculating the PV of both the bond's FV and the coupon payment (C) in each period can be summarized as:

$$PV = C \div (1+i)^1 + C \div (1+i)^2 + \ldots \ C \div (1+i)^t + \ FV \div (1+i)^t$$

Again, 'i' is the quoted interest rate or yield, and 't' is the maturity period (t = 1, 2, ..., 30 years). Since the PV is to be received at a date certain in the future (i.e., period 't'), it is the highest price that one would pay in the current period to buy the bond.

When using MarketSim you and other participants are assigned specific periods for playing the game. The beginning (end) of a period to the beginning (end) of the next period is equivalent to a year in terms of calculating the bond yield. Consequently, in any given period, the yield that you must offer in order to sell a bond that matures within the period increases as the remaining time in that period decreases. For example, if you issue or sell a bond whose FV is $100 for a SP of $91 at the beginning of a period the interest to the buyer is $9, which is equivalent to a yield of about 10% (9.89%) assuming that the bond matures at the beginning of the next period. On the other hand, if you issue the bond at the same price of $91 in the middle of the current period and it matures at the end of the period the yield will be approximately 21%.

In every period, you should note the following stipulations as you play the game.

1. As you approach the close of a period feel free to cancel any outstanding offer that remains since the yield that you might have to pay in order to sell the bond will be too high.

2. In your role as a producer, you or your firm should issue new bonds in the primary markets when you need to buy more capital. Doing so is a commitment to pay the FV of the bond but by using the borrowed funds to buy capital you can produce more goods and consequently make more profits—part of which you also use to pay for the interest cost on the bonds. Also, by reselling existing bonds in your portfolio, you can generate cash quickly for use in a variety ways such as hiring more labor or making dividend payments to households.

3. In your role as a consumer, buying bonds now is a way of preserving a part your current income (or cash) and will allow you to increase your future consumption as the bonds mature. However, deferring too much consumption in the current period might actually lower your lifetime utility. Therefore, try to spread your consumption more or less evenly over

the entire game.

The following examples illustrate how to calculate Present Value (PV) to determine the selling/purchasing price of a bond. Example 1 highlights the relationship between the bond price and the face value of the bond. Example 2 demonstrates how MarketSim calculates the PV.

Example 1: PV and the Relationship between Bond Price and its Face Value

1. Consider a pure discount bond that has a face value of $100,000. Suppose the interest rate is 5%. What will this bond sell for in this period if:

    a. the maturity date is one year?

    Solutions: $PV = FV \div (1+i)^t = \$100,000 \div (1+.05)^1 = \$95,238.10$

    This is the most price that a potential buyer would willing to pay for this bond.

    b. the maturity date is three years?

    Solutions: $PV = FV \div (1+i)3 = \$100,000 \div (1+.05)3 = \$86,383.76$

    This is the most price that a potential buyer would be willing to pay for this bond

---

Example 2: PV and the Relationship between Bond Price and its Face Value As Implemented in MarketSim.

As mentioned earlier, chances are that you will not trade in bonds immediately at the start of a period. This means that a bond might actually mature within one period instead of the next period that would coincide exactly with one full maturity period (or a year) from a theoretical view point. The consequences of trading within a specific period are higher (1) bond yield, and (2) selling price. The following numerical examples illustrate both cases.

Suppose you want to sell a bond that has a FV = $100, and a yield (i) = 10%.

1. What is the selling price if you were to sell the bond at the beginning of the current period and the bond matures exactly in one full period—that is, it matures at the exact time at the beginning of the next period?

Solution: SP or $PV = \$100 \div (1+.10)^1 = \$90.90$ or **$91**

2. What is the SP you would set if you wanted to sell the bond halfway into the current period and the bond matures at the end of the same period?

Solution: SP or PV $= \$100 \div (1+.10)^{\frac{1}{2}} = \$95.4919 = \mathbf{\$95.50}$

Notice that the SP is higher than it otherwise would have been had the bond matured in one full period.

3. What is the bond yield (**i**) if the SP = \$91, the bond is sold halfway into the current period and it matures at the end of the same period?

Solution: Because both the FV and the SP are known, the PV rule can be used to solve for 'i' as follows:

$$\$91 = 100 \div (1+.i)^{\frac{1}{2}}$$
$$\text{or } [\$91(1+.i)^{\frac{1}{2}}]^2 = 100^2$$
$$\text{or } 91^2(1+.i) = 10,000$$
$$\text{or } 8281(1+i) = 10,000$$

Isolating 'i' yields **i = 21%** (.20758) which is higher than the yield (10%) had the bond matured in one full period or year. This is why the yield that the MarketSim reports might not be exactly the same as the one you are likely to obtain by using the PV formula to determine the selling price of bond with a fixed maturity date, 't'.

Activity 1: Understanding the structure of the 'Firm Bond Market Actions' page.
Click on the "Bonds" link under the "Firm" to open the page.

1. Taking Stock of your firm's Portfolio
A.
    i. How many Bonds do you currently hold?
    ii. What is the FV, the maturity period, and the yield of each bond?
B.
    i. If any, how many of your bonds are still outstanding?
    ii. What is the FV, the maturity period, and the yield of each bond?
C. Suppose your cash on hand is \$100, and your firm's outstanding bond (face value = \$200) is designated to mature at the end of the current period. What will happen to

i.   inventory value
ii. capital value, and
iii. why does the program make the changes?

2. Concepts Relating to Issuing Bonds: Use Figure 62

Figure 62: Issuing a New Bond

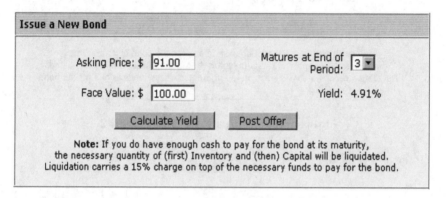

A. Complete the missing information for the posted bond.
i.   The principal or face value is $
ii. The selling price is $
iii. The yield is
iv. The maturity date is

Activity 2: Using the Firm Bonds Page to Borrow Money (offer to issue Bonds)

A. Assume you are going to offer a bond with a face value of $100 and an asking price of $91. In Figures 63 and 64, compare the value of the yield and explain why they differ.

Figure 63: Issuing a New Bond, yield 1

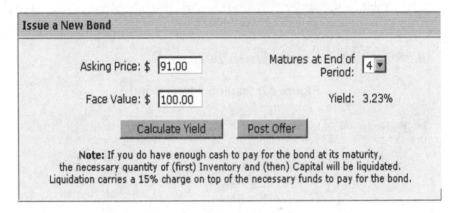

Issue a New Bond

Asking Price: $ [91.00]   Matures at End of Period: [4 ▼]

Face Value: $ [100.00]   Yield: 3.23%

[Calculate Yield]   [Post Offer]

Note: If you do have enough cash to pay for the bond at its maturity, the necessary quantity of (first) Inventory and (then) Capital will be liquidated. Liquidation carries a 15% charge on top of the necessary funds to pay for the bond.

Figure 64: Issuing a New Bond, yield 2

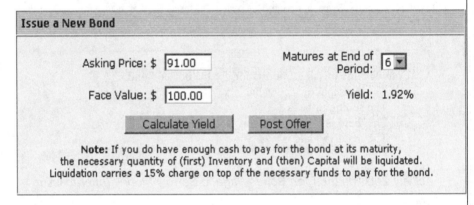

Issue a New Bond

Asking Price: $ [91.00]   Matures at End of Period: [6 ▼]

Face Value: $ [100.00]   Yield: 1.92%

[Calculate Yield]   [Post Offer]

Note: If you do have enough cash to pay for the bond at its maturity, the necessary quantity of (first) Inventory and (then) Capital will be liquidated. Liquidation carries a 15% charge on top of the necessary funds to pay for the bond.

Activity 3: Bond Yield and Asking Price (offer to re-sell Bonds)
Assume you are at the very beginning of period 5 and you are holding a bond with a face value of $210 that matures at the end of period 6. Table 18 shows the possible asking prices and their corresponding yields to the potential buyer:

Table 18

Asking price	110	140	170	200
Yield (to buyer)	38.17%	22.47%	11.14%	2.47%

A. Describe in a sentence the relationship between the asking price and the corresponding yield to the potential buyer.

B. As a seller:
   i. which yield is the most attractive?
   ii. why might it not be possible to sell the bond at that price?.

C. As a potential buyer, which yield is the most attractive? Explain.

Activity 4: Using the Consumer Bonds Page to Sell Bonds

Assume you are at the very beginning of period 3 and you are holding a bond with a face value of $320 that matures at the end of period 5. Table 19 shows the possible asking prices and their corresponding yields to the potential buyer.

Table 19

Asking price	225	250	275	300
Yield (to buyer)	12.46%	8.58%	5.18%	2.17%

A. Describe in a sentence the relationship between the asking price and the corresponding yield to the potential buyer.

B. As a seller:
   i. which yield is the most attractive?
   ii. why might it not be possible to sell the bond at that price?.

C. As a potential buyer, which yield is the most attractive? Explain.